Past Masters
General Editor Keith Thomas

Thomas More

Past Masters

AQUINAS Anthony Kenny
ARISTOTLE Jonathan Barnes
BACH Denis Arnold
FRANCIS BACON Anthony
   Quinton
BAYLE Elisabeth Labrousse
BERKELEY J. O. Urmson
THE BUDDHA Michael Carrithers
BURKE C. B. Macpherson
CARLYLE A. L. Le Quesne
CHAUCER George Kane
CLAUSEWITZ Michael Howard
COBBETT Raymond Williams
COLERIDGE Richard Holmes
CONFUCIUS Raymond Dawson
DANTE George Holmes
DARWIN Jonathan Howard
DIDEROT Peter France
GEORGE ELIOT Rosemary Ashton
ENGELS Terrell Carver
GALILEO Stillman Drake
GOETHE T. J. Reed

HEGEL Peter Singer
HOMER Jasper Griffin
HUME A. J. Ayer
JESUS Humphrey Carpenter
KANT Roger Scruton
LAMARCK L. J. Jordanova
LEIBNIZ G. MacDonald Ross
LOCKE John Dunn
MACHIAVELLI Quentin Skinner
MARX Peter Singer
MENDEL Vitezslav Orel
MONTAIGNE Peter Burke
THOMAS MORE Anthony Kenny
WILLIAM MORRIS Peter Stansky
MUHAMMAD Michael Cook
NEWMAN Owen Chadwick
PASCAL Alban Krailsheimer
PETRARCH Nicholas Mann
PLATO R. M. Hare
PROUST Derwent May
TOLSTOY Henry Gifford

Forthcoming

AUGUSTINE Henry Chadwick
BAGEHOT Colin Matthew
BERGSON Leszek Kolakowski
JOSEPH BUTLER R. G. Frey
CERVANTES P. E. Russell
COPERNICUS Owen Gingerich
DESCARTES Tom Sorell
DISRAELI John Vincent
ERASMUS John McConica
GIBBON J. W. Burrow
GODWIN Alan Ryan
HERZEN Aileen Kelly
JEFFERSON Jack P. Greene
JOHNSON Pat Rogers
KIERKEGAARD Patrick Gardiner
LEONARDO E. H. Gombrich

LINNAEUS W. T. Stearn
MILL William Thomas
MONTESQUIEU Judith Shklar
NEWTON P. M. Rattansi
ROUSSEAU Robert Wokler
RUSKIN George P. Landow
RUSSELL John G. Slater
SHAKESPEARE Germaine Greer
ADAM SMITH D. D. Raphael
SOCRATES Bernard Williams
SPINOZA Roger Scruton
VICO Peter Burke
VIRGIL Jasper Griffin
WYCLIF Anthony Kenny

and others

Anthony Kenny

Thomas More

Oxford   New York

OXFORD UNIVERSITY PRESS

Oxford University Press, Walton Street, Oxford OX2 6DP
London New York Toronto
Delhi Bombay Calcutta Madras Karachi
Kuala Lumpur Singapore Hong Kong Tokyo
Nairobi Dar es Salaam Cape Town
Melbourne Auckland
and associated companies in
Beirut Berlin Ibadan Mexico City Nicosia

Oxford is a trade mark of Oxford University Press

First published 1983 as an Oxford University Press paperback
and simultaneously in a hardback edition
Hardback reprinted with corrections 1985

British Library Cataloguing in Publication Data
Kenny, Anthony
Thomas More. (Past masters)
1. More, Sir Thomas, Saint 2. Philosophy
I. Title II. Series
192 B785.M8
ISBN 0–19–287574–4
ISBN 0–19–287573–6 Pbk

Library of Congress Cataloging in Publication Data
Kenny, Anthony John Patrick.
Thomas More. – (Past masters)
Bibliography: p. Includes index.
1. More, Thomas, Sir, Saint, 1478–1535. 2. Great
Britain – History – Henry VIII, 1509–1547.
3. Statesmen – Great Britain – Biography.
4. Christian saints – England – Biography.
I. Title. II. Series.
DA334.M8K46 1983 942.05'2'0924 [B] 83–4209
ISBN 0–19–287574–4
ISBN 0–19–287573–6 (pbk.)

Set by Colset Pte Ltd, Singapore
Printed in Great Britain by
Antony Rowe Ltd., Chippenham

Acknowledgements

I am indebted to Fr. J. McConica, Dr John Guy, Dr Maurice Keen, Mr G. Watson, Mr Keith Thomas and Dr Henry Hardy for assistance on various points in connection with the writing of this book.

Contents

Note on abbreviations

The following abbreviations are used in references given in the text:

D   *Dialogue of Comfort against Tribulation*, ed. Manley

E   *The Essential Thomas More*, ed. Greene and Dolan

H   Harpsfield's Life of More (Everyman)

L   *St Thomas More: Selected Letters*, ed. Rogers

R   Roper's Life of More (Everyman)

U   *Utopia*, ed. Surtz

W 1 and 2 *The English Works of Sir Thomas More*, ed. Campbell and Reed

Y   *The Yale Edition of the Complete Works of St Thomas More.*

Full bibliographical details of these and other works are given in the suggestions for further reading at the end of the book.

Introduction

Thomas More deserves a place in the intellectual history of Europe for three reasons. He wrote a Latin classic, *Utopia*, which is as widely read today as ever. In his life he set a particular pattern of scholarship, saintliness and public service which has continued to fascinate writers and historians of many different kinds, and which contributed to the standard English conception of the English character. His voluminous English writings occupy a significant place in the history of the language and of its controversial and devotional literature. These three claims on the historian of ideas are of unequal weight, and there would be no agreement among scholars about the order in which they should be placed. But the three claims must be considered together if More's significance is to be fairly assessed; and for this reason a Past Master on More must treat of his life and death as well as of the ideas he committed to paper.

Utopia can indeed be read and enjoyed even by those who know nothing of its author's life. It has given pleasure to many generations, whether it has been read as an account of a newly discovered continent (as it was by some of More's contemporaries), or as a light-hearted frolic of the imagination with no serious purpose other than satire (as it still is by some of More's Catholic co-religionists), or as a serious political and economic programme for setting up a communist society, written by a man of genius who 'championed the oppressed classes even when he stood alone' (as it was by the pioneer socialist Karl Kautsky). To begin to understand the book– ironic as it is in parts – it is enough to know that it is a product of the energetic drive for reform characteristic of the best Catholic scholars before the Protestant Reformation made their advocacy of change more qualified and more cautious.

But the reading of *Utopia* is enlightened by new insight, and darkened by new problems, when the reader realises that its author took an active part in the political life of the corrupt society he satirises, was prepared to die for doctrines flatly contradictory to those which the book seems to hold out for admiration, and helped put men to death for deviations from Catholic orthodoxy far less serious than those of the Utopians. An acquaintance with More's life and an understanding of his stance in controversy is not something extraneous to an intelligent reading of *Utopia*: it is essential to its correct interpretation.

Despite More's deep involvement in the religious battles of the age, he has often been admired as a pattern of erudition and integrity by the heirs of his opponents. No one has ever claimed him as a great statesman; but he is often held up, and not only by Catholics, as the pattern of an incorruptible judge and an unservile courtier. For Samuel Johnson he was 'the person of greatest virtue these islands ever produced'. Robert Southey, in *Colloquies on Society*, conjures his spirit from the grave as an embodiment of wisdom. For C. S. Lewis, More was 'a man before whom the best of us must stand uncovered'.

In the earliest biographies, and to a lesser extent in his own English writings, More appears as a man of uncommon wit and cheerfulness. His jokes, unlike most early Tudor jokes, are sill pointed and amusing. More, indeed, is the first person to embody the peculiarly English ideal that the good man meets adversity and crisis not with silent resignation, nor with a sublime statement of principle, but with a joke. One of More's most recent biographers has very well said, 'More was never more witty than when he was least amused.' More was,

I believe, the first person systematically to use wit to greet dangerous and desperate situations in a way that was later taken to express a characteristically English sang-froid throughout the country's history up to the Somme and the Battle of Britain. Something of the same style was to be observed in antiquity, from Socrates to Saint Laurence; but I know of no real-life Englishman to embody it so fully before More, though something of it is to be found in the fictional characters of Chaucer.

The charm and virtues of More naturally posed a conundrum for those historians who regarded his stand in religious controversy as backward and perverse. Macaulay can serve as a spokesman for many: he offers the case of More as a proof that religion and theology are not progressive disciplines like the sciences.

> We have no security for the future against the prevalence of any theological error that has prevailed in time past. . . When we reflect that Sir Thomas More was ready to die for the doctrine of transubstantiation, we cannot but feel some doubt whether the doctrine of transubstantiation may not triumph over all opposition. More was a man of eminent talents. He had all the information on the subject that we have, or that, while the world lasts, any human being will have. . . We are therefore unable to understand why what Sir Thomas More believed respecting transubstantiation may not be believed to the end of time by men equal in abilities and honesty to Sir Thomas More. But Sir Thomas More is one of the choice specimens of human wisdom and virtue; and the doctrine of transubstantiation is a kind of proof charge. A faith which stands that test will stand any test.

More's works of controversy are indeed the most equivocal

of his legacies to the republic of letters. Even among Roman Catholics few read today, for the sake of their content, his defences of the doctrinal, sacramental and legal system of medieval Christendom. They would certainly never have been reprinted in recent years had they not been the work of the author of *Utopia* and the martyr of Tower Hill. Yet they cannot be entirely passed over by the historian of ideas. After all, the intellectual system of Western Christianity was one to which all the choicest minds had contributed for centuries: and More's defence of it is the fullest statement in English of the points of conflict between the traditional system and the Reformers who sought to break it. But More contributed little of his own to the system he defended; and so his English works have caught the attention less of historians of theology than of historians of the language.

Dr Johnson, in the 'History of the English Language' prefaced to his Dictionary, prints copious extracts from More's prose and verse, on the ground that 'it appears from Ben Jonson that his works were considered as models of pure and elegant style'. In the early part of the present century a grammarian wrote, 'whatever the language was when More found it, where he left it, there it remained until Dryden definitely civilized it'. Recent writers have been much more critical of his style and sceptical of his influence on the language. But C. S. Lewis, who is as severe on More the writer as he is in awe of More the man, repeatedly praises him as a comic writer and story-teller: his 'merry tales', he tells us, 'will bear comparison with anything of the same kind in Chaucer or Shakespeare'.

More's devotional writings have a much wider appeal than his controversial tracts. The noblest of these is the *Dialogue of Comfort*, written during his imprisonment at the end of his life. No one who shares the religious premises on which the book is based can read it without admiration; and those who reject the premises cannot remain unmoved by an encounter with the unblinking and cheerful manner in which More meditates on the prospect of pain and death.

In the present book I have tried to do justice, so far as its small compass allows, to the three aspects of More's importance for the intellectual and moral history of our culture. I have set out the principal ideas of *Utopia* and offered an interpretation of its message; I have told the story of More's life so far as is necessary to indicate the impact of his personality on later admirers and to illustrate the wit of his spoken words; I have sketched the Catholic system that he was defending and given specimens of the energetic style in which he couched his defence. I have tried, finally, to show that the scholar, the martyred public servant, and the controversial prose writer are not three different, conflicting personalities, but a single, consistent human being.

1 The young humanist

Thomas More was born in the last years of the reign of Edward IV, a King of that Yorkish dynasty whose bloody feuds with the House of Lancaster are known as the Wars of the Roses. In 1483, when Thomas was about five, King Edward died, leaving the throne to his thirteen-year-old son, Edward V. Within the year young Edward was dead and his uncle, the Duke of Gloucester, became King as Richard III. Thirty years later More became Richard's first biographer: it was he who first told at length the story of the murder in the Tower of London of Edward and his young brother at the orders of their wicked uncle. Two years later Richard himself was slain, defeated in the final battle of the Wars of the Roses by the Lancastrian claimant, Henry Tudor, who succeeded as King Henry VII.

It was during the twenty-four-year reign of Henry VII that More grew from boyhood to manhood. He was the son of John More, a barrister of Lincoln's Inn, whose family lived in the parish of St. Lawrence Jewry in the City of London. After schooling at St. Anthony's in Threadneedle Street, Thomas became a page to the Archbishop of Canterbury at Lambeth Palace. The Archbishop, John Morton, was Henry VII's Lord Chancellor and became a Cardinal: in his household the boy waited on the leading statesmen and ecclesiastics of the age. Visitors admired his precocious conversation, and remembered how wittily he improvised at Christmas stage-plays. 'This child here waiting at table,' the Cardinal is reported to have said, 'whosoever shall live to see it, will prove a marvellous man' (R 3).

On Morton's advice Thomas More was sent, in his early teens, to study at Oxford, perhaps to Canterbury College (now Christ Church), perhaps to Magdalen College School. The Master at Magdalen School was John Holt, tutor to the pages in Cardinal Morton's household; he published a text-book of grammar to which the adolescent More contributed a prologue and an epilogue in Latin verse. More was at Oxford less than two years altogether. He did not treasure his time there, and does not seem to have made many lifelong friends: the only one known to have been his Oxford contemporary is Cuthbert Tunstall of Balliol. In later years More recalls the poor fare of Oxford, and often mocks at the logic taught there. Most of his own scholarship he acquired after he went down from the University.

John More was anxious that his son should follow him in a legal career, and brought him back to London to qualify as soon as possible. Thomas entered one of the Inns of Chancery for preparatory training and went on to be admitted to Lincoln's Inn on 12 February 1496 (the first certain date of his career). He progressed steadily and was called to the Bar about 1502. In addition to his own legal studies he taught younger lawyers at Furnivall's Inn, and mastered ancient Latin literature so well that he was invited to give a course of lectures on St. Augustine's *City of God* in the church of St. Lawrence Jewry. The Rector there was William Grocyn, one of the very few scholars in England to know Greek. In 1501 More began to study the language with him and soon became competent enough to produce elegant Latin versions of diffi-cult Greek epigrams. By the time that he was twenty-five he was, though a lawyer by profession, one of the most accom-plished classical scholars of his generation.

The age in which More grew up was one of discovery and rediscovery. It was in the year that he first went to Oxford that

Christopher Columbus discovered America. The study of the Greek and Latin literature of pagan antiquity had impassioned scholars in Italy for several decades; it had been given a fillip by the arrival of refugee Greek scholars when the Turks sacked Constantinople in 1453. This renaissance of classical learning was now spreading from Italy northwards through Europe: one of the greatest scholars of the age was a Dutch priest, Desiderius Erasmus, who met More on a visit to England in 1499 and soon became one of his closest friends.

Erasmus and his circle became known as 'humanists'. This did not mean that they desired to replace religious values with secular human ones: it meant that they believed in the educational value of the 'humane letters' or Greek and Latin classics. Humanists turned away from the technical, logical and philosophical studies which had preoccupied so many scholars during the later Middle Ages – the so-called 'scholastic' philosophy – and placed new emphasis on the study of grammar and rhetoric. They communicated with each other in Latin, and strove to write elegant prose on the model of the most admired authors of ancient Rome, instead of using the medieval lingua franca, which they condemned as barbaric. New philological methods were developed by them to establish sound and accurate texts of the ancient writers. These texts were published in handsome editions by the new printer-publishers who were exploiting the recently developed art of printing. Humanists believed that the tools of their scholarship, applied to the ancient pagan texts, would restore to Europe long-forgotten arts and sciences, and, applied to the texts of the Bible and of ancient Christian writers, would help Christendom to a purer and more authentic understanding of Christian truths.

The revival of letters was accompanied by a general flowering of culture. More lived at the climax of Renaissance art:

Michelangelo was three years his senior, and Raphael five years his junior. The artistic renaissance, too, crossed the channel to England: it was a colleague of Michelangelo's who designed the tomb of Henry VII in Westminster.

In matters of religion, the Europe in which More grew up was a single whole. Britain, France, Germany, Spain, Italy and Austria alike consisted of Catholic States which acknowledged the central authority of the Pope, the Bishop of Rome. But the supremacy of the Papacy, and the unity of Christendom, had suffered a series of wounds which, in More's lifetime, were to prove fatal. For the greater part of the fourteenth century the Popes lived not at Rome but at Avignon in France. It was a scandal that the first bishop of Christendom should set an example of absenteeism, and in addition the Avignon Popes became notorious for extortionate taxation of the faithful. The return of the Papacy to Rome was followed in 1378 by the outbreak of the Great Schism: for nearly forty years the church had not one Pope but two, one in Rome and one in Avignon, each supported by half of Christendom, and each calling the other an impostor. The schism did not end until a General Council of the Church at Constance in 1417 elected Pope Martin V. The way in which the schism was ended left many Christians in doubt whether the supreme authority in the Church lay with Pope Martin and his successors, or with General Councils in succession to Constance. The Popes of the fifteenth century, moreover, acted less as universal pastors than as local Italian princes; in aggrandisement of their own families some of them did not shrink from bribery, warfare and assassination, and the ecclesiastical counterparts of these crimes, simony, interdict and excommunication. The Pope under whom Thomas More grew from boyhood to manhood was Alexander VI (1492–1503), the most villainous man ever to have occupied the Roman See.

More will have learnt as a child, of course, the lesson which he was later to repeat in controversy with Protestants, that the sacredness of an office is not destroyed by the unworthiness of its holder. Someone growing up in England, in any case, did not encounter ecclesiastical scandal on the gigantic scale found in the Church in Italy. English bishops, in the main, were worldly rather than wicked; English monasteries, for the most part, were comfortable rather than corrupt. Many of the high clergy were civil servants who derived their emoluments from church benefices; they paid impoverished substitutes to perform their pastoral duties. Dominican and Franciscan friars, whose vocation obliged them to live on alms, had once been admired for their zeal and poverty; they were now regarded by many, with greater or less justice, as idle parasites. But the parochial clergy remained popular enough, and the English people as a whole were reputed by foreigners to be devout. 'They attend Mass every day', wrote a Venetian traveller in 1497, 'and say many Paternosters in public, the women carrying long rosaries in their hands.'

The profound importance of the Church to English people was manifest above all in the seven sacraments, or official ceremonies, which marked the main events, and catered for the spiritual needs, in the lives of the faithful from womb to tomb: baptism in infancy, confirmation in childhood, matrimony and holy orders to inaugurate a secular or clerical vocation, penance and eucharist to cleanse and feed the soul, the last anointing to comfort the sick and dying. The provision of the sacraments was the major function of the institutional Church, and the sacraments were essential if the believer was to achieve the holiness of life, or at the very least the holiness at the hour of death, which was needed to gain eternal life in heaven and avoid eternal punishment in hell. Such was the orthodoxy against which in England, since the time of the fourteenth-century Lollards, hardly any heretical voices had for long been raised.

England was devout, and free from overt heresy; but no Englishman had been canonised as a Saint since Thomas of Hereford, who died in 1282. Yet amid the easygoing, cosy Catholicism of the majority there were communities where holy men and women lived severe lives of poverty, of chastity and of obedience to a rigorous rule. One such was the London Charterhouse, where Carthusian monks lived in silent contemplation in solitary cells. More was attracted to this austere vocation; during his legal training he lived in or near the Charterhouse for four years, sharing in the monastic life of fasting and prayer. While writing his lectures on St. Augustine, Erasmus tells us, More was almost resolved to become a priest, 'but, as he found he could not overcome his desire for a wife, he decided to be a faithful husband rather than an unfaithful priest'. But even after he married, More continued to practise monastic austerities, wearing a hair shirt beneath his clothes as a penitential garment. 'He used also', his son-in-law records, 'sometimes to punish his body with whips, the cords knotted, which was known only to my wife, his eldest daughter, whom for her secrecy above all other he specially trusted, causing her, as need required, to wash the same shirt of hair' (R 25). Several of the London Carthusians were, like More, to meet a martyr's death: as he watched them going to their execution from his window in the Tower, More, talking to his daughter, compared the happy lot of these religious, who after a life of penance went to their deaths like bridegrooms to their marriage, with 'such as have, in the world, like worldly wretches, as thy poor father have done, consumed all their time in pleasure and ease licentiously' (R 39).

At no time did More live in a way that a man of the world would have regarded as licentious. An epigram or two survives to tell of youthful love affairs. 'He showed no aversion to women, but he destroyed no one's good name,' Erasmus tells us. 'In fact he was always rather the tempted than the tempter and found more pleasure in the intercourse of mind than of body' (E 290). When More was about twenty-six he decided to marry. He was a regular visitor at the house of John Colt, a wealthy landowner living in Essex, who had three handsome daughters. More, according to his son-in-law, was most attracted by the second, as 'the fairest and best favoured'; 'yet when he considered that it would be both great grief and some shame also to the eldest to see her younger sister in marriage preferred before her, he then of a certain pity framed his fancy towards her and soon after married her' (R 4). More settled his wife Jane at a house called The Old Barge in Bucklersbury. He at once took her education in hand, doing his best to interest her in literature and music. Jane's progress was slow and tearful; she resented being catechised after the Sunday sermon. Besides, she had little time for learning, since in four years of marriage she bore four children, Margaret, Elizabeth, Cecily and John. But Erasmus, who was a regular visitor to the household in Bucklersbury, describes it as a happy and affectionate one. Jane, he tells us, was growing into an ideal intellectual companion for More when she died, still in her early twenties.

In the year of his marriage More was elected to Parliament. The Parliament was a brief one, summoned to grant a special feudal levy to King Henry VII. More denounced the King's demand as excessive, and the Parliament voted less than half the sum requested. The King was told that 'a beardless boy had disappointed all his purpose'. By his action, More forfeited all chance of royal favour and preferment for the rest of the reign; he would never again oppose a royal will so swiftly and incautiously. When, five years later, the King died and was succeeded by his eighteen-year-old son Henry VIII, More, like many other Englishmen, greeted the news with delight. He celebrated the coronation in Latin verse, contrasting the young King's virtues with the avarice and extortion that had characterised the previous reign:

> Now serfhood is fast bound, here's freedom's spring;
> Sadness is at an end, and joy's before.
> The youth today anointed England's king
> The age's splendour is for ever more. (E 120)

Henry was crowned on 24 June 1509 with Catherine of Aragon, his newly married Queen. Catherine had come to England in 1501 and married Henry's elder brother, Arthur Prince of Wales, but the Prince had died a year later. Henry, as her brother-in-law, was forbidden by church law to marry her: a dispensation to permit the marriage had to be obtained from Pope Julius II, who had succeeded Alexander VI in 1503.

A year after Henry's accession, in September 1510, More was appointed under-sheriff of London. His duties were to give legal advice to the sheriffs, and to sit as judge on Thursday mornings in the Guildhall. For these duties, and from fees for representing the City and his private clients in the courts at Westminster, the young lawyer was soon earning the substantial sum of £400 a year.

A number of literary works, both English and Latin, survive from these early years of More's life. At about the time of his marriage he translated a life of Giovanni Pico della Mirandola, an austere Florentine scholar and philosopher, now some ten years dead. More admired 'Picus' as a model for the life of a devout layman. He translated into English verse several of Pico's writings, including 'The twelve properties of a lover', of which the tenth runs as follows:

> The lover is of colour dead and pale;
> There will no sleep into his eyes stalk;
> He favoureth neither meat, wine, nor ale;
> He mindeth not what men about him talk;

But eat he, drink he, sit, lie down or walk,
He burneth ever as it were with a fire
In the fervent heat of his desire.

Here should the lover of God ensample take
To have him continually in remembrance,
With him in prayer and meditation wake,
While other play, revel, sing and dance:
None earthly joy, disport, or vain pleasance
Should him delight, or anything remove
His ardent mind from God, his heavenly love.

(W 1.393)

More light-hearted were the verses entitled 'A merry jest how a sergeant would learn to play the friar', a jingling story, written perhaps for a lawyer's junket, about a sergeant who, to serve an arrest upon a bankrupt, disguised himself as a friar. Once admitted in his charitable disguise, the sergeant revealed himself

And out he took his mace
Thou shalt obey
Come on thy way
I have thee in my clutch
Thou goest not hence
For all the pence
The mayor hath in his pouch. (E 166)

There follows much boisterous description of knockabout farce. But the poem has a serious message: each man must stick to his trade. For

When a hatter
Will go smatter
In philosophy

> Or a pedlar
> Wax a medlar
> In theology (E 159)

nothing will go well.

More wrote English verses also on the ages of man, and on the tricks of fortune. In collaboration with Erasmus, he translated into Latin some of the works of the Greek satirist Lucian. These, published in 1506, sold in his lifetime best of all his works, being reprinted at least thirteen times.

Jane More died in the summer of 1511 shortly after giving birth to her fourth child. More married again within the month. His haste was not the fruit of any romantic passion: 'he rather married', we are told, 'for the ruling and governing of his children, house and family, than for any bodily pleasure' (H 105). His bride was Alice Middleton, a prosperous merchant's widow, who brought into the family a solid dowry. More's friends did not like Dame Alice; some called her 'aged, blunt and rude', and another could no longer bear to stay in the house because of her 'harpy's hooked nose'. More himself is said to have called her, ungallantly, 'neither a pearl nor a girl' (E 291). Most of the wives who figure in the 'merry tales' sprinkled through More's works are shrews; many biographers, no doubt rashly, have taken these figures as portraits of Dame Alice. It is clear from the earliest biographies that More habitually addressed his wife in a tone of affectionate teasing, rather than with the intellectual seriousness he used with his daughter Margaret. He did not try to interest his second wife, like his first, in literature: he contented himself with encouraging her to sing to the lute and zither. When More composed an epitaph for his first wife's tomb he praised Alice for being an affectionate stepmother to Jane's children; he could not tell, he said, which of his two wives was more greatly beloved: 'How fine it could have been if fate and religion had allowed us all three to live together.'

Besides More's children by Jane, his household now contained his new wife's daughter Alice (later Lady Alington), and his adopted daughter Margaret Gigs. It was soon extended by the addition of two infant wards, Anne Cresacre and Giles Heron. Wardships in Tudor times were often purchased as an investment, and these two wardships brought More a considerable income. But the two wards fitted happily into the family: Anne Cresacre married More's son John, and Giles married his daughter Cecily.

It was in the early years of his marriage that More wrote his first substantial prose work: a life of Richard III. He worked on two versions of it, one English and one Latin; neither was ever finished, and both were published, incomplete, after his death. The book has been described as the first serious historical biography in English; scholars are not agreed whether it gives an accurate portrait of the King. But the picture it draws of a monster of wickedness has taken an irrevocable hold on the popular historical imagination. This is because it lies, at one remove, behind Shakespeare's *Richard III*. Here is More's description of the killing of the princes in the Tower at the behest of the usurping King.

Sir James Tyrell devised that they should be murdered in their beds. To the execution whereof, he appointed Miles Forrest, one of the four that kept them, a fellow fleshed in murder beforetime. To him he joined one John Dighton, his own horsekeeper, a big, broad, square, strong knave. Then, all the others being removed from them, this Miles Forrest and John Dighton, about midnight (the silly children lying in their beds) came into the chamber and suddenly lapped them up among the clothes, so bewrapped them and entangled them, keeping down by force the feather bed and pillows hard into their mouths, that within a while, smothered and stifled, their breath failing, they gave up to God their innocent souls into the joys of heaven, leaving to their tormentors their bodies dead in the bed. Which after that the wretches perceived, first by the struggling with the pains of death, and after long lying still, to be thoroughly dead: they laid their bodies naked out upon the bed, and fetched Sir James to see them. Which, upon the sight of them, caused these murderers to bury them at the stair foot, meetly deep in the ground, under a great heap of stones. Then rode Sir James in great haste to King Richard, and showed him all the manner of the murder; who gave him great thanks, and, as some say, there made him knight. (W 1.450)

The Latin version of Richard III, it has been conjectured, may have been written for Erasmus. Certainly Erasmus continued as a regular guest in More's household after his second marriage, and a devoted correspondent throughout life. In 1511 he dedicated to More a light-hearted work, *The Praise of Folly*, with the punning Latin title *Encomium Moriae*. Some theologians pulled long faces at the mocking tone of the book: More took up his pen to defend Erasmus's underlying seriousness of purpose. This was shown abundantly when, in 1516, Erasmus published his pioneering edition of the Greek New Testament. The firsthand study of the Bible in the original languages, More and Erasmus believed, was worth much more than the textbook knowledge of contemporary theologians who parroted medieval commentators. But opposition to the new kind of scholarship was deeply felt. More, who was to become High Steward of the University of Oxford, had to write to the University in 1518 to defend the study of Greek against a series of attacks from lecturers and preachers. Of course, he wrote, a man might be saved without knowing Latin and Greek: but even worldly learning prepares the mind for virtue. Theology itself cannot be mastered without knowledge of Hebrew, Greek and Latin: it is vain to boast of a knowledge of Scripture and the Fathers if one is not master of the language in which they are written. More must have been gratified when a readership in Greek was set up at Corpus Christi College: doubly gratified when the reader chosen was John Clement, his children's tutor, who was later to marry his adopted daughter Margaret Gigs.

Among More's children, natural and adopted, girls outnumbered boys by six to two. All were given, at home, careful schooling in religion, classical literature and humanistic learning. More hired a series of tutors to teach his children and, in due course, his grandchildren. In a letter to one of these tutors, William Gonell, he urges the importance of training his daughters in virtues as well as in letters: 'for erudition in women is a new thing and a reproach to the idleness of men' so that, if a woman proves vicious, slanderers will attack female education 'and blame on letters the faults of nature, using the vices of the learned to make their ignorance count as virtue'. But if a woman combines virtue with letters, 'she will have more real benefit than if she added the riches of Croesus to the beauty of Helen' (L 103). More wrote his children Latin letters, of which a few have survived, some in prose and some in verse: he expected a letter in return from each of them, almost daily – quite a feat of Latin composition for young schoolchildren. Besides Latin the children learnt Greek, logic, philosophy, theology, mathematics and astronomy. The first textbook of arithmetic to be published in England – *On the art of Calculation*, by More's friend Tunstall – was dedicated to More 'to be passed on to your children'.

More's favourite and most accomplished daughter was his

eldest, Margaret. He was proud of the beautiful Latin she wrote and would show off her letters to his learned friends; she and her sisters won praise even from the fastidious Erasmus. More's household was a paradigm of humanist enlightenment, and a pioneering venture in the higher education of women.

2 The commonwealth of Utopia

The year 1515 was a turning-point in More's life. In that year he was given by the King his first important commission, and he wrote the most famous of his works. With Tunstall, he was sent to Flanders to negotiate the interpretation of treaties of Henry VII governing the wool and cloth trade. Erasmus gave the ambassadors a letter of introduction to Peter Gilles, the town clerk of Antwerp. The months of negotiations left More the leisure to write the greater part of a work entitled *Utopia*. As we have it, the work is a dialogue between More, Gilles and a fictitious traveller named Raphael Hythlodaye, a companion of the navigator Amerigo Vespucci from whom the newly discovered continent of America took its name. The major part of the dialogue is a description by Hythlodaye of the distant commonwealth of Utopia, or Nowhereland. Like Plato's *Republic* before it, and the many Utopian constitutions devised since, More's *Utopia* uses the depiction of an imaginary nation as a vehicle for theories of political philosophy and criticism of contemporary political institutions. Like Plato, More often leaves his readers to guess how far the arrangements he describes are serious political proposals and how far they merely present a mocking mirror to reveal the distortions of real-life societies. The description of Utopia was complete when More returned to England in 1515; at home he added an introductory dialogue, which became book one of the final *Utopia*. But it is the second book which is the heart of the work.

Utopia is an island, shaped like a crescent moon, five hundred miles long and two hundred across at its broadest part. It contains fifty-four cities, each surrounded by twenty miles or so of agricultural land. Throughout the country there are farms, each containing, as well as a pair of serfs, a household of forty free men and women. These are city-dwellers who have been sent into the country for a two-year stint of farming. Twenty are sent each year by rota: they spend a year learning husbandry from their predecessors and another teaching it to their successors.

All the cities resemble each other in laws, customs and institutions. Each year three elders from each city meet in a Senate in the capital, Amaurot. In size, shape and situation Amaurot, as described by More, resembles the London of his day. But in one respect Amaurot is startlingly different: there is no such thing there as privacy or private property. The terraced houses back on to spacious gardens; the doors to the houses and through them to the gardens swing open easily and are never locked. 'Whoso will, may go in, for there is nothing within the houses that is private, or any man's own. And every tenth year they change their houses by lot' (U 65).

In each city, every group of thirty households elects annually a magistrate called a Syphogrant; there are altogether two hundred of these per city. Each group of ten Syphogrants, with their households, is ruled by a Tranibore, another elected annual magistrate. The Tranibores form the Council of the supreme magistrate or Prince, who is chosen for life by the Syphogrants from a panel elected by popular vote. Whenever the Council meets, two Syphogrants must be present, a different pair each day. Nothing can be decided until it has been debated for three days, and it is a capital offence to discuss State matters outside the Council. This is to prevent the princes and Tranibores from changing the republic into a tyranny. Matters of particular importance are laid before all the assembled Syphogrants, but nothing is decided until they have had time to consult their several households. On rare occasions matters may be laid before the Senate of the whole island.

Every citizen learns agriculture, first in school, and then during a turn of duty on the farm. In addition every citizen, male or female, is taught a particular craft, such as cloth-making, masonry, metalworking or carpentry. Utopia is unlike Europe, where differences of class and status are marked by elaborate distinctions in dress; people all wear the same clothes, except for a distinction between the sexes and between the married and the unmarried. All clothes are home-made in each household.

No one is allowed to be idle, and all must work every day at their crafts, overseen by a Syphogrant. Citizens can choose their crafts, but if they wish to specialise in a craft other than their father's, they must transfer to a household dedicated to that craft. The working day is brief: Utopians work for three hours before noon, rest for two hours after dinner, and then work a further three hours before supper. They go to bed at eight and sleep for eight hours: the hours of early morning and evening are thus leisure time to be spent as each pleases. In the morning there are public lectures, compulsory for those citizens who have been assigned as scholars, optional for others, male or female. The evening may be spent in music or in conversation, or in chess-like games in which numbers devour numbers, or virtues battle in panoply against vices.

How do the Utopians manage to satisfy all their needs while working so many fewer hours than Europeans? You can easily work this out, if you consider how many people in Europe live idly:

First, almost all women which be the half of the whole number: or else, if the women be somewhere occupied, there most commonly in their stead the men be idle.

Besides this, how great and how idle a company is there of priests and religious men, as they call them; put thereto all rich men, specially all landed men, which commonly be called gentlemen and noblemen – take into this number also their servants: I mean all that flock of stout bragging swashbucklers. Join to them also sturdy and valiant beggars, cloaking their idle life under the colour of some disease or sickness. (U 71–2)

Even among the few real workers in Europe, many spend their time producing superfluous luxuries rather than the things which are necessary for survival, comfort or natural pleasures. No wonder, then, that in Utopia where no more than five hundred able-bodied persons in each city-state are dispensed from manual labour, a six-hour day suffices.

Dispensations are given, by the Syphogrants, on the advice of the priests, only to those who seem specially fitted for learning and scholarship. From this small class of scholars are chosen the Utopian priests, Tranibores and Princes. Syphogrants need not be scholars, but they too are exempted by law from labour; they take no advantage of this privilege, however, so as to set others an example of work.

The work in Utopia is made light, not only by the many hands, but by the simplicity of the needs they serve. The buildings, being all communal property, do not suffer from private neglect, nor are they being continually altered at the whim of new owners. The manufacture of clothes calls for no great labour, since Utopians prefer coarse and sturdy wear of undyed cloth.

Occasionally the citizens are summoned from their regular crafts to perform large-scale public works, such as the mending of highways. On other occasions, when the economy is thriving, a public proclamation will shorten the working day. The magistrates do not weary their citizens with superfluous labour; the keynote of their policy is this: 'What time may possibly be spared from the necessary occupations and affairs of the commonwealth, all that the citizens should withdraw from the bodily service to the free liberty of the mind, and garnishing of the same. For herein they suppose the felicity of this life to consist' (U 75).

In More's Utopia, unlike Plato's Republic, the primary social unit is the family or household. Girls, when they grow up, move to the household to which their husbands belong; but sons and grandsons remain in the same household under the rule of the oldest parent until he reaches his dotage and is succeeded by the next oldest. The size of the households is strictly controlled. The number of births is not regulated, nor the number of children under fourteen; but no household may include less than ten or more than sixteen children who have grown up. The excess children in the larger households are moved to households where there are less than the minimum. If the number of households in the whole city grows beyond the statutory limit of six thousand, families are transferred to smaller cities. If every city in the whole island is already fully manned a colony is planted in unoccupied land overseas. If the natives there are unwilling to join them, and resist their settlement, the Utopians will establish the colony by force of arms; 'for they count this the most just cause of war, when any people holdeth a piece of ground void and vacant to no good or profitable use, keeping others from the use and possession of it which, notwithstanding, by the law of nature, ought thereof to be nourished and relieved' (U 76). If any of the homeland cities become dangerously undermanned, as has sometimes happened in time of plague, the Utopian colonists are recalled from abroad to make up the lack.

Each household, as explained earlier, will be devoted to a single craft. The products of the household's labour are placed in storehouses in the market-place in the centre of the quarter to which the household belongs. Every householder can carry away from these storehouses, free of charge, anything which he and his family need. In their dealings with each other, the Utopians make no use at all of money.

> For why should anything be denied unto anyone, seeing there is abundance of all things, and that it is not to be feared lest any man will ask more than he needeth? For why should it be thought that a man would ask more than enough, who is sure never to lack? Certainly, in all kinds of living creatures, either fear of lack doth cause covetousness and greed, or, in man only, pride, which counteth it a glorious thing to pass and excel others in the superfluous and vain ostentation of things. The which kind of vice among the Utopians can have no place. (U 77)

Food, likewise, is distributed freely to every household which needs it: but individual householders have to wait their turn until food has been allotted first of all to the hospitals, on the prescription of doctors, and secondly to the houses of the Syphogrants. These houses contain great halls large enough to contain the whole of the thirty households making up the Syphograncy. Here, at dinner-time and supper-time, a brazen trumpet summons all the households to a communal meal. No one is forbidden to eat at home, but it is frowned on and almost nobody does so. 'It were a folly to take the pain to dress a bad dinner at home, when they may be welcome to good and fine fare so nigh hand at the hall' (U 79).

The women of the households take turns to prepare the food and arrange the meals, but they leave the menial and dirty kitchen tasks to the serfs. The tables are set against the walls, as in European monasteries and colleges: the men sit with their backs to the walls, the women on the other side so that they can leave the table easily if they feel unwell or need to attend to a child. The nursing mothers – and Utopian women nurse their own children whenever possible – eat apart with the under-fives in a nursery, which is a 'certain parlour appointed and deputed to the same purpose never without fire and clean water, nor yet without cradles; that when they will, they may down the young infants, and at their pleasure take them out of their swathing clothes, and hold them to the fire, and refresh them with play' (U 80). The children over five wait at table, or if they are too young to do so 'they stand by with marvellous silence', having food passed to them from the tables. At every table the diners sit 'four to a mess', as they do to this day in the Inns of Court. The Syphogrant and his wife, and the most senior citizens, sit at a high table on a dais, just like the Benchers of an Inn. They are joined, if there is a church in the Syphograncy, by the priest and his wife.

Both dinner and supper begin with a brief reading from an edifying book; after that, conversation is allowed, and it is specially noted that the elderly are not allowed to monopolise the time with long and tedious talk, but must provoke the young to speak, 'that they may have a proof of every man's wit, and towardness, or disposition to virtue; which commonly in the liberty of feasting, doth shew and utter itself'. Supper lasts longer than dinner, because the working day is over.

No supper is passed without music. Nor their banquets want no conceits, nor junkets. They burn sweet gums and spices or perfumes, and pleasant smells, and sprinkle about sweet ointments and waters, yea, they have nothing undone that maketh for the cherishing of the company. For they be much inclined to this opinion: to think no kind of pleasure forbidden, whereof cometh no harm. (U 81)

Travelling in Utopia is carefully regulated. To go from one

city-state to another a passport is needed from the Tranibores stating the duration of the absence, and no one is permitted to travel alone. A free ox-cart, with a serf to drive, is provided; but Utopians rarely take advantage of this. For they do not need to carry provisions, since on arriving in another city-state they stay with the members of their profession and work at their crafts just as if they were at home. Travel between city-states without a passport is severely punished, and for a second offence a citizen can be reduced to serfdom. Within the same city-state a man does not need a passport to travel in the country, only 'the good will of his father and the consent of his wife'. But wherever he is, he must do a morning's work before he is given dinner, and an afternoon's work if he is to be given supper. This all ensures that no one is idle, no one goes hungry, and no one needs to beg.

The Utopians travel overseas to trade with other nations: they will export grain, honey, wool, hides, livestock and the like once thay have provided two years' supply of everything for themselves. When their ships arrive abroad, they distribute one-seventh of their cargoes to the poor of the country; the rest they sell at moderate prices. Though the Utopians do not use money among themselves, they need it for a number of international purposes. Iron, gold and silver are their main imports; they use exports principally to build up credit, to be drawn on to make loans to other people or to wage war. As a provision for time of war, they keep a large treasury at home to bribe enemy nationals or to hire mercenaries ('they had rather put strangers in jeopardy than their own countrymen').

Among the most astonishing things about Utopia are the arrangements for preserving the treasury of precious metals. The Utopians see, justly, that iron is of much greater real value than the precious metals. So they are careful not to set any artificial value on gold and silver. They do not lock them away, or work them into fine plate which they would be loath to part with in emergencies. Instead:

> Whereas they eat and drink in earthen and glass vessels – which indeed be curiously and properly made, and yet be of very small value – of gold and silver they make chamber pots and other vessels that serve for most vile uses; not only in their common halls, but in every man's private houses. Furthermore, of the same metals they make great chains, fetters, and gyves, wherein they tie their bondmen. Finally, whosoever for any offence be disgraced, by their ears they hang rings of gold: upon their fingers they wear rings of gold; and around their neck chains of gold: and, in conclusion their heads be tied with gold. (U 86)

Pearls, diamonds and rubies are cut and polished and given to children to keep with their rattles and dolls.

Hythlodaye recalls that during his visit to Utopia there arrived an embassy from the distant land of Anemolia. The Anemolian ambassadors, ignorant of Utopian customs, sought to impress their hosts by the gorgeousness of their apparel. They wore cloth of gold, and gold necklaces, finger-rings and ear-rings, and caps flashing with pearls and gems. The Utopians took the most simply attired servants to be the leaders of the embassy; the ambassadors they mistook for slaves because of the gold that weighted them down. 'Look, mother,' said one Utopian child, 'there is a great grown fool wearing pearls and jewels as if he were a little boy.' 'Hush, child,' said the mother, 'I think he is one of the ambassador's jesters.' After a few days in Utopia the ambassadors learnt their mistake, and laid aside their fine gear. 'We marvel', the Utopians explained, 'that any men be so foolish as to have delight and pleasure in the doubtful glistering of a little trifling stone, when they may behold any of the stars, and the sun itself' (U 88).

Just as the Utopians despise those who take pleasure in jewellery, so too they regard it as madness to take pride in courtly honours. 'What natural or true pleasure', they ask, 'does thou take of another man's bare head, or bowed knees? Will this ease the pain of thy knees, or remedy the frenzy in thine own head?' (U 96). Likewise, they cannot understand how men can find pleasure in casting dice upon a table, or hearing dogs bark and howl after a hare. What pleasure is there in seeing dogs run?

> But if the hope of slaughter, and the expectation of tearing in pieces the beast, doth please thee, thou shouldest rather be moved with pity to see a silly innocent hare murdered of a dog: the weak of the stronger; the fearful of the fierce; the innocent of the cruel and unmerciful. (U 98)

So the Utopians regard the cruel sport of hunting as unworthy of free men. Even the slaughter of animals which is necessary for food is not permitted to citizens: only serfs are allowed to become butchers; because through the killing of beasts, they maintain, 'clemency, the gentlest affection of our nature' (U 98), decays and perishes little by little.

Though they despise cruel sports, the Utopians enjoy and delight in the pleasures of the body and of the senses, and take pride and joy in their unparalleled health and strength. They are no ascetics, and indeed regard as perverse bodily mortification for its own sake.

> To despise the comeliness of beauty, to waste the bodily strength, to turn nimbleness into slothness, to consume and make feeble the body with fasting, to do injury to health, and to reject the pleasant motions of nature . . . for a vain shadow of virtue, for the wealth and profit of no man, to punish himself, or to the intent he may be able courageously to suffer adversity, which perchance shall never come to him – this to do, they think it a point of extreme madness, and a token of

a man cruelly minded towards himself, and unkind towards nature. (U 102)

But it is the pleasures of the mind, rather than of the body, which most delight the Utopians. Though only a few citizens are dispensed from labour to devote themselves entirely to study, all are taught letters (in their own vernacular) and most men and women devote their leisure throughout life to reading. Before Hythlodaye's visit they were ignorant of Greek and Latin literature, but had made as much progress in music, logic, arithmetic and geometry as any of the classical authors. They were ignorant of modern (that is, medieval) logic, and of astrology; and very much better so. But when they heard a description of Greek literature they were anxious to learn the language; and those who were chosen to do so mastered it within the space of three years. They were delighted to accept from Hythlodaye a fine library of classical texts in Renaissance editions. Indeed, printing and paper-making were the only two European arts which the Utopians envied. Here too they proved quick learners, and acquired both skills in a short time.

In describing the customs of Utopia mention has been made from time to time of serfs. Serfdom is not hereditary slavery: most serfs are Utopians or foreigners reduced to serfdom as punishment for the kind of crime which is elsewhere punishable by death. When Utopians take prisoners in war, they use them as serfs; but they do not buy the prisoners of others as slaves. Labourers from other countries, finding Utopian serfdom preferable to their own drudgery, sometimes become serfs voluntarily; these are given lighter work, and are allowed to return home if ever they please to do so.

The sick are well cared for by the Utopians, who pride themselves on the enlightened and sanitary design of their hospitals. They sit with the incurably diseased and comfort them by every possible means.

But if the disease be not only uncurable, but also full of continual pain and anguish, the priests and the magistrates exhort the man, seeing he is not able to do any duty of life, and by overliving his own death, is noisome and irksome to others and grievous to himself, that he will determine with himself no longer to cherish that pestilent and painful disease. And seeing his life is to him but a torment, that he will not be unwilling to die, but rather to take a good hope to him, and either dispatch himself out of that pain, as out of a prison, or a rack of torment, or else suffer himself willingly to be rid out of it by others. (U 108)

Such a suicide is regarded as a virtuous and noble action; but if a man kills himself without the advice of the priests and the magistrates, he is regarded as unworthy either to be buried or cremated; 'they cast him unburied into some stinking marsh' (U 109).

The marriage customs of the Utopians have attracted, or shocked, many of the book's readers. Men marry at twenty-two, and women at eighteen. Those convicted of premarital intercourse are forbidden to marry without a special pardon from the prince, and the heads of their household are disgraced. If promiscuity were allowed, the Utopians say, few would be willing to accept the burdens of monogamous matrimony.

Hythlodaye reports the custom observed by the Utopians in choosing wives and husbands.

A grave and honest matron sheweth the woman, be she maid or widow, naked to the wooer: and likewise a sage and discreet man exhibiteth the wooer naked to the woman. At this custom we laughed, and disallowed it as foolish. But they on the other part do greatly wonder at the folly of all other nations, which in buying a colt (whereas a little money is in hazard) be so chary and circumspect, that although he be almost all bare, yet they will not buy him, unless the saddle and all the harness be taken off; lest under those coverings be hid some gall or sore. And yet in choosing a wife, which shall be either pleasure or displeasure to them all their life after, they be so reckless that all the residue of the woman's body being covered with clothes, they esteem her scarcely by one hand breadth (for they can see no more but her face), and so do join her to them, not without great jeopardy of evil agreeing together if anything in her body afterward should chance to offend and mislike them. (U 110)

No doubt, after a marriage is consummated a body may wither or decay; in that case there is no remedy but patience. But before marriage no one should be allowed to conceal deformity beneath deceitful clothes.

Unlike most of their neighbours, the Utopians are monogamous, and marriage is in principle lifelong. However, adultery may break a marriage; the innocent, but not the adulterous, spouse is allowed to remarry. Besides adultery, 'the intolerable wayward manners of either party' provide grounds for divorce and the remarriage of the unoffending spouse. On rare occasions divorce by consent is permitted.

Now and then it chanceth, whereas the man and woman cannot well agree between themselves, both of them finding other with whom they hope to live more quietly and merrily, that they, by the full consent of them both, be divorced asunder and married again to others. But that not without the authority of the Council: which agreeth to no divorces before they and their wives have diligently tried and examined the matter. Yea, and then also they be loth to consent to it; because they know this to be the next way to break love between man and wife – to be in easy hope of a new marriage! (U 111)

Adultery is punished with serfdom, and divorce follows auto-
matically unless the guiltless spouse is prepared to share the
bondage and drudgery. (Such selfless devotion sometimes wins
pardon for the guilty party.) Death is the punishment for
repeated adultery: the only crime so punished, other than
rebellion by those already condemned to serfdom. Minor
matrimonial offences of wives are punished by husbands; the
use of cosmetics is regarded as wanton pride, for beauty is less
esteemed than probity. 'As love is sometimes won with beauty,
so it is not kept, preserved, and continued, but by virtue and
obedience' (U 111).

Apart from the laws governing marriage, there is little to be
told about Utopian municipal law, because of the lack of private property. Altogether, the Utopians have very few laws;
they despise the massive tomes of laws and commentaries to be
found in other countries. 'They think it against all right and
justice, that men should be bound to laws which either be in
number more than be able to be read, or else blinder and darker
than that any man can well understand them' (U 114). Their
own laws are simple, and always given the most obvious interpretation. This enables them to dispense altogether with
lawyers: they think it better that a man should plead his own
case, and tell the same story to the judge that he would tell to his
attorney.

The Utopians' virtues have inspired their neighbours to
invite Utopian proconsuls to govern them, ruling for a
five-year period and then returning home. Such officials are
untempted by bribes (for what good is money to them, since
they will shortly be returning to a country where it is not used?)
and undeflected by malice or partiality (since they are living
among strangers). So the two vices which most corrupt
commonwealths are absent from the Utopians' allies.

Though the Utopians have allies and friends among other

nations, they make no treaties or leagues. If man and man will not league together by nature, the words of treaties will not make them do so, they argue.

> They be brought into this opinion chiefly because, that, in these parts of the world leagues between princes be wont to be kept and observed very slenderly. For here in Europe, and especially in these parts where the faith and religion of Christ reigneth, the majesty of leagues is every where esteemed holy and inviolable: partly through the justice and goodness of princes, and partly at the reverence and motion of the Sovereign Pontiffs. Which, like as they make no promise themselves, but they do very religiously perform the same, so they exhort all princes in any wise to abide by their promises; and them that refuse or deny so to do, by their pontifical power and authority, they compel thereto. (U 116)

More's irony reveals the degree of contempt into which the pontifical government had been brought, even among loyal Catholics, by the perfidious behaviour of Alexander VI and Julius II. The readiness of rulers to break treaties, he goes on, makes men think that justice is a virtue which is far too plebeian for kings to practise; or at least

> that there be two justices: the one meet for the inferior sort of the people; going a-foot and creeping low by the ground, and bound down on every side with many bands; the other, a princely virtue; which, like as it is of much higher majesty than the other poor justice, so also it is of much more liberty; as to the which, nothing is unlawful that it lusteth after. (U 117)

Unlike other nations, the Utopians do not regard war as anything glorious; but they are not pacifists either. Both men and women receive regular military training, and they regard war as justified to repel invaders from their own or friendly territory, to liberate peoples oppressed by tyranny, to avenge injustices done to their allies. Pecuniary losses abroad to their own citizens they do not regard as justifying war; but if a Utopian is wrongfully disabled or killed anywhere, they first send an embassy to inquire into the facts, and if the wrongdoers are not surrendered they forthwith declare war. They prefer to win wars by stratagem and cunning than by battle and bloodshed, glorying in victories won by gifts of intellect rather than by the strength and powers that men share with animals.

Their one aim in war is to secure the object which, if it had been granted beforehand, would have prevented the declaration of war; or else, if that is impossible, to punish those at fault so as to deter future wrongdoing. One of their methods of minimising bloodshed is this. When war is declared, they cause posters to be set up secretly throughout enemy territory offering great rewards for the assassination of the enemy king, and smaller but still considerable sums for the deaths of other named individuals, regarded as responsible for the hostilities. This spreads dissension and distrust among the enemy; but it also means that those most likely to be killed in a war are not the general guiltless mass of the enemy nation, but the few wrongdoers among their leaders. For they know that common people do not go to war of their own wills, but are driven to it by the madness of rulers.

When battles do have to be fought abroad, the Utopians employ mercenaries: the fierce, rough Zapoletans, who live in rugged mountains like the Swiss Alps, hardy people who have no trade but fighting and care about nothing but money. Since the Utopians have so much gold, they can outbid rivals in purchasing Zapoletans. Only a small contingent of their own citizens is sent abroad, to accompany the commander and his deputies; and no one is enlisted for foreign service unless he volunteers. If Utopia itself is invaded, however, then all are placed in the front line, on shipboard or on the ramparts, brave men and fainthearts together, men and women alongside each other.

> In set field the wives do stand every one by their own husband's side; also every man is compassed next about with his own children and kinsfolk . . . It is a great reproach and dishonesty for the husband to come home without his wife, or the wife without her husband, or the son without his father. (U 125)

This gives the Utopians unparalleled courage and spirit in battle.

In each battle, as in war generally, the main aim is to destroy the leadership: a band of picked youths is bound by oath to seek out and kill or capture the opposing general. Once the battle is won there is no disordered pursuit or indiscriminate slaughter: the Utopians prefer to take prisoners than to kill the vanquished. They keep truces religiously, and they injure no noncombatants except spies; they never plunder captured cities, but the defeated are obliged to bear the expense of the war once it is over.

The final part of Hythlodaye's account of Utopia concerns religion. Some in Utopia worship heavenly bodies, or departed heroes; but the great majority there believe 'that there is a certain godly power, unknown, everlasting, incomprehensible, inexplicable, far above the capacity and reach of man's wit,' which they call 'the father of all' (U 130). The medley of Utopian superstitions is gradually giving way to the worship of this single supreme being; but the majority do not impose their religious beliefs on others. The founder of Utopia, seeing that religious divisions were a great source of discord,

> made a decree that it should be lawful for every man to favour and follow what religion he would; and that he might do the

best he could to bring others to his opinion, so that he did it peaceably, gently, quietly and soberly; without hasty and contentious rebuking and inveighing against others. If he could not by fair and gentle speech induce them unto his opinions, yet he should use no kind of violence and refrain from displeasant and seditious words. To him that would vehemently and fervently in this cause strive and contend, was decreed banishment or bondage. (U 133)

There was one Utopian who became a convert to Christianity, and proselytised offensively with excessive zeal, consigning all non-Christians to everlasting fire. He was arrested, tried and banished, 'not as a despiser of religion, but as a seditious person and raiser up of dissension among the people' (U 133).

The tolerance proclaimed by the founder of Utopia was no mere device for keeping the peace: he thought it might well be true that God inspired different men with different beliefs so that he might be honoured with a varied and manifold worship. Even if only a single religion were true and the rest superstitions, truth is best left to emerge by its own natural strength. But Utopian religious toleration has its limits. It is regarded as base and inhuman to believe that the soul perishes with the body; anyone who professes such an opinion is treated as untrustworthy, excluded from public office and forbidden to defend his belief in public. Those who err on the opposite side, and attribute immortal souls to non-human animals, are left in peace.

Utopians believe not only in immortality, but in a blissful afterlife. For this reason, though they lament illness, they do not regard death, in itself, as an evil. Reluctance to die they take as a sign of a guilty conscience; one who obeys the summons of death with reluctance is viewed with horror and carried out to burial in sorrowful silence. But those who die cheerfully are not buried but cremated amid songs of joy. 'And in the same place they set up a pillar of stone, with the dead man's titles therein graved. When they be come home, they rehearse his virtuous manners and his good deeds. But no part of his life is so oft or gladly talked of, as his merry death' (U 136).

The Utopians believe that the dead revisit their friends invisibly and move above the living as witnesses of all their words and deeds. Thus they feel protected as they go about their business, but also deterred from any secret misdoing.

We have seen that the Utopians despise asceticism for its own sake. None the less, there are groups among them who live selfless lives embracing tasks which are rejected as loathsome by others, giving up their leisure to tend the sick, or undertake public works on roads or in field or forest. Some of these people practise celibacy and vegetarianism; others eat flesh, live normal family lives and avoid no pleasure unless it gets in the way of their work. The Utopians regard the former sect as holier but the second sect as wiser.

The Utopians, we are told, have priests of extraordinary holiness 'and therefore very few'. There are thirteen in each city under a bishop, all elected by popular vote in secret ballot. They preside over worship and conduct services, but are also censors of morals: to be rebuked by the priests is a great disgrace. The clergy are not authorised to inflict any punishment other than exclusion from divine service; but this punishment is dreaded more than almost any other.

Women as well as men may become priests, but they are chosen only if they are widows of a certain age. The male priests marry the choicest wives. The priests, male and female, have charge of the education of children and young people. No Utopian court may punish them for any crime. In battle they kneel beside the fighting armies, 'praying first of all for peace, next for victory of their own part, but to neither part a bloody victory'. When victory comes they mingle with their own victorious armies, restraining the fury and cruelty of the soldiers. They have averted such slaughter that their reputation is high among all neighbouring nations. 'There was never any nation so fierce, so cruel and rude, but they had them in such reverence, that they counted their bodies hallowed and sanctified, and therefore not to be violently and unreverently touched' (U 142).

Hythlodaye's narrative of the Utopians concludes with a minute description of the feasts with which they keep holy the first and last days of the month and the year, to offer thanks for prosperity past and pray for prosperity future. All family quarrels are reconciled before the feasts; 'if they know themselves to bear any hatred or grudge towards any man, they presume not to come to the sacrifices before they have reconciled themselves and purged their consciences' (U 143). The priests wear vestments made of birds' feathers, like those of American Indian chiefs. The service ends with a solemn prayer in which the worshippers thank God that they belong to the happiest commonwealth and profess the truest of all religions. The worshipper adds that if he is in error in believing this, 'if there be any other better than either of them is, being more acceptable to God, he desireth him that he will of his goodness let him have knowledge thereof, as one that is ready to follow what way soever he will lead him' (U 145).

3 The King's councillor

The first book of *Utopia* was written after the second, and it is much less Utopian: instead of describing the constitution of an imaginary republic, it weighs the pros and cons of entering public service in real-life monarchies. It seems, indeed, to have been written to clear More's own mind when he was wondering whether he should become an official of Henry VIII. On the one hand, his own career hitherto pointed in that direction: the very embassy to Flanders out of which *Utopia* grew was an earnest of future royal employment. More's father and many of his humanist friends, including Tunstall, had already joined the Royal Council. On the other hand, Erasmus and some other humanists thought scholars had no business to enter public service, where the Court could corrupt them, and the needs of policy compromise their independent principles.

In *Utopia*, the case against royal service is made by Hythlodaye; the case in favour of it is made by the More of the dialogue. Service to kings, Hythlodaye suggests, is little better than slavery: why should a scholar give up his ease for it, when kings are only interested in war-making? Hythlodaye recalls his own firsthand experience of the English Court in the time of Cardinal Morton. He relates a long and spirited denunciation of the rapacity of the English upper classes, whose unscrupulous greed and passion for luxury destroy the livelihood of the poor and make them first starve, and then steal, and then hang for stealing. No one took any serious notice of that: they all just watched to see the Cardinal's reaction. More too can recall Morton's court from his days as a page there, but he reminds Hythlodaye that Plato believed that common-wealths could only be happy if either philosophers become kings, or kings turn to philosophy. How far off happiness is if philosophers will not even condescend to give advice to kings!

Plato was no doubt right, Hythlodaye says, to think that kings would never take philosophers' advice unless they became philosophers themselves. Plato himself, at the court of Sicily, found how useless it was for a philosopher to offer advice to an unphilosophical king. If Hythlodaye were to offer good advice to contemporary monarchs, it would fall on ears as deaf as Plato's did. There is no room for philosophy with rulers.

That may be true of scholastic philosophy, More says: but it is possible to adapt philosophy for statesmen. 'If evil opinions and naughty persuasions cannot be utterly and quite plucked out of their heart, if you cannot even as you would, remedy vices which use and custom have confirmed; yet for this cause you must not leave and forsake the commonwealth: you must not forsake the ship in a tempest, because you cannot rule and keep down the winds' (U 50). It is fruitless to try to convert rulers to a wholly new way of thinking;

> but you must with a crafty wile and subtle train study and endeavour yourself, as much as in you lieth, to handle the matter wittily and handsomely for the purpose, and that which you cannot turn to good, so to order it that it be not very bad: for it is not possible for all things to be well, unless all men were good; which I think will not be yet these good many years. (U 50)

Such dissembling is dishonourable, says Hythlodaye; only radical change will do any good. Where there is money and private property there can be no justice or true prosperity in the commonwealth. More doubts whether if the profit motive

were altogether removed there could be enough goods produced. That, says Hythlodaye, is because More has never
seen Utopia; which he proceeds to describe in the second book
which was summarised in our previous chapter.

In the dialogue, Hythlodaye is given the last word: but in
the event, More seems to have been more convinced by the
arguments he puts in his own mouth. By August 1517 he had
accepted an invitation to join the King's Council, though he
did not dare to tell Erasmus until nearly a year later. He
allowed Erasmus to believe, rightly or wrongly, that he had
accepted the invitation with great reluctance. King Henry
could not rest, Erasmus wrote, until he dragged More to
court – literally dragged 'because no one has ever been as
eager to get into court as More was to stay out of it' (E 292).

More's first employment as councillor was a modest
embassy to Calais in 1517 to settle a commercial dispute
between English and French merchants. His effective
superior was Thomas Wolsey, Archbishop of York and Cardinal, who for the next twelve years was Henry VIII's Lord
Chancellor and the leading figure in English politics. Wolsey
controlled the Council, which the King rarely attended; only a
handful of councillors accompanied the King as the Court
moved around the country. More took part in the work of the
Council at Westminster, but much of his time in the royal
service was spent in the King's household as it travelled. The
King often sent for him, to discuss astronomy, geometry or
divinity with him, as well as public affairs; at night time he
would invite him on to the roof 'to consider with him the
diversities, courses, motions and operations of the stars and
planets'. More was called so frequently to entertain the King
and Queen that he could not get away from court more than
two days together in a month: he had 'to dissemble his nature'
and to 'disuse himself of his former accustomed mirth'

until they let him go home to his wife and children (R 7).

More's household was now growing. In 1521 Margaret More married William Roper, twelve years her senior, son of a family friend of the Mores and now a student of Lincoln's Inn. John Aubrey, in his *Brief Life* of More, tells the story of Roper's wooing thus:

> He came one morning, pretty early, to my Lord, with a proposal to marry one of his daughters. My Lord's daughters were then both together abed in a truckle-bed in their father's chamber asleep. He carries Sir William into the chamber and takes the sheete by the corner and suddenly whippes it off. They lay on their Backs, and their smocks up as high as their armepitts. This awakened them, and immediately they turned on their bellies. Quoth Roper, I have seen both sides, and so gave a patt on the buttock he made choice of sayeing, Thou art mine. Here was all the trouble of the wooeing.

Aubrey says he had the tale from the granddaughter of one of Roper's cronies, but it is more likely derived from the provisions in *Utopia* for premarital inspection.

Roper came to live in More's household, and later became his first (and still his best) biographer. Margaret Roper was soon pregnant, and More wrote happily to her in the expectation of his first grandchild:

> May God and our Blessed Lady grant you happily and safely an addition to your family like to his mother in everything except sex. Let it indeed be a girl, if she will make up for the disadvantage of her sex by her zeal to imitate her mother's virtue and learning. I would most certainly prefer such a girl to three boys. (L 155)

Even an intimate note of this kind was written in Latin, and

Margaret was not to let her family duties interrupt her studies. Writing in the early days of her marriage More said, 'I earnestly hope that you will devote the rest of your life to medical science and sacred literature' (L 149), and he concluded by urging her to overtake her husband in the study of astronomy.

A year or two after the Ropers' marriage More moved his household from the City centre to a thirty-four-acre farm on the river at Chelsea, where now Battersea Bridge joins Cheyne Walk. He constructed a mansion there with a separate building in the garden containing a chapel, and a library as a hideaway for himself. In 1526 the painter Hans Holbein visited Chelsea: he described the house as 'dignified without being magnificent'. He was commissioned to paint a series of family portraits and a family group. Sketches for the portraits are now at Windsor Castle and a draft of the family group is at Basle. The painting itself survives only in copies, but they and the sketches give a picture of the Chelsea household which is familiar to millions.

Among the many visitors to Chelsea was the King himself. An admirer of learning who shared More's enthusiasm for the education of women, Henry was impressed when More's three daughters engaged each other in formal philosophical disputation. Roper recalls the King's visits: there was one in particular which dwelt in his mind.

> For the pleasure he took in his company, would His Grace suddenly sometimes come home to his house in Chelsea, to be merry with him; whither on a time, unlooked for, he came to dinner to him, and after dinner, in a fair garden of his, walked with him by the space of an hour, holding his arm about his neck. As soon as His Grace was gone I, rejoicing thereat, told Sir Thomas More how happy he was whom the King had so familiarly entertained . . . 'I thank

our Lord, son,' quoth he, 'I find His Grace my very good lord indeed, and I believe he doth as singularly favour me as any subject within this Realm. Howbeit, son Roper, I may tell thee I have no cause to be proud thereof, for if my head could win him a castle in France (for then was there war between us) it should not fail to go.' (R 12)

More was at this time in constant service on the King as Royal Secretary. He was a valuable intermediary between Henry and Wolsey because he was almost the only man they both trusted. Wolsey was anxious to bring impartial justice within the reach of poor as well as rich in England, and he professed himself a lover of international peace. The author of *Utopia* was attracted by both these goals: as things turned out, he was able to contribute much more to the former than to the latter. On his travels with the King he dealt with bills of complaint brought to the itinerant court; in Westminster he sat as judge in the Star Chamber, Wolsey's chosen means to expedite and simplify litigation. At discussions of foreign policy in the council he was forced to observe that Wolsey's projects for peace took second place to Henry's ambition for military glory.

The shifts and turns of Wolsey's foreign policy involved More in a number of diplomatic ventures. In 1520 he accompanied Henry to meet Francis I of France at the Field of the Cloth of Gold, a sumptuous pageant at which the two kings swore eternal friendship; a year later he accompanied Wolsey to Calais on a mission which led to an alliance against Francis with the Emperor Charles V. He found his work in England more useful and congenial than a diplomatic career, and he later refused to undertake an embassy to Spain.

In 1523, when war broke out with France, a Parliament was summoned to raise the necessary taxes: More, by now a Knight, and Under-Treasurer of the Exchequer, was chosen Speaker, Wolsey demanded a tax of four shillings in the pound, but the Commons resisted this heavy imposition. Wolsey appeared in person to press the demand, and asked each member in turn his opinion. None would reply: the custom was for the Speaker to be their mouthpiece in dealing with the King or his representative.

'And thereupon he required an answer of Master Speaker, who first reverently upon his knees excusing the silence of the House, abashed at the presence of so noble a personage, able to amaze the wisest and best learned in a Realm', went on to defend the custom that 'for them to make answer was it neither expedient nor agreeable with the ancient liberty of the House'. Nor could he reply himself: true, they had all trusted him to be their voice; 'yet except everyone of them could put into his one head all their several wits, he alone in so weighty a matter was unmeet to make His Grace answer' (R 10). Four months later the Commons voted three shillings in the pound instead of four, over a period of years instead of a lump sum.

Wolsey was not pleased with More. ' "Would God" ', he said to him one day in his Whitehall gallery, ' "you had been at Rome, Master More, when I made you Speaker." "Your Grace is not offended, so would I too, my Lord," quoth he' (R 11).

More's career as Speaker had not been undignified; but the raising of heavy taxes to support war between Christian princes was not the kind of royal service for which the author of *Utopia* had left the leisure of the scholar.

Publicly, however, More's relations with Wolsey remained cordial as long as Wolsey remained in power. When peace was made in 1525 More was one of the signatories of the Treaty, which brought the French, the English and Pope Clement VII into league with each other against the Emperor. The Pope gained little from this alliance: Rome was twice sacked by the Emperor's armies. Henry was unwilling to spend more than words in support of the Pope. It fell to More, as Secretary, to write the letters of consolation: 'I trust I have so couched and qualified them', he wrote to Wolsey, 'that they shall be to the satisfaction of the Pope's holiness and such other as shall hear and read the same, without binding the King to anything that might redound to his charge.' The King did, however, send More and Wolsey to France in 1527 to encourage the French to mount an expedition to rescue the Pope. For Henry now had a reason of his own for wanting the goodwill of Clement.

By 1527 Henry had grown tired of his marriage with Catherine of Aragon. He had, it will be recalled, married her as his brother's widow, with a dispensation from Pope Julius II. After eighteen years of marriage he had still no male heir: Princess Mary was the only survivor of a series of miscarriages, still births and cot deaths. If he died without a male heir the kingdom might return to the chaos of the Wars of the Roses. His attention was drawn by someone to the words of Leviticus: 'He that marrieth his brother's wife doth an unlawful thing. . . they shall be without children.' Beside these reasons of State and conscience, more pressing reasons of the heart made Henry anxious to terminate his marriage. Some time in 1527 he had fallen in love with a maid-of-honour, Ann Boleyn, the younger sister of a former mistress. Unlike her sister, Ann was unwilling to admit the King to her favours without at least the prospect of becoming Queen.

Could it be claimed that Pope Julius's dispensation was invalid, *ultra vires* because against the text of Leviticus? If so, the marriage with Catherine was no marriage, and Henry was free to marry Ann. But the matter was complicated. Was it certain that the marriage between Catherine and Arthur had ever been consummated? Was there not a text of

Deuteronomy to set against that of Leviticus? Was it likely that Clement VII would overrule his predecessor's decision, thus calling in question the dispensing power of the Papacy? Moreover, Catherine was aunt to the Emperor Charles V: and in the year after the sack of Rome Clement knew well the price of incurring the Emperor's displeasure.

The King decided, however, that it was worth while to seek an annulment of the marriage. He caused himself to be cited before Cardinal Wolsey's court for having lived in incest for eighteen years. He sought the advice of his bishops, including the poorest and holiest of them, John Fisher of Rochester. Fisher replied, guardedly, that he saw no reason to believe that the dispensation granted by Pope Julius was beyond the Papal powers.

When More returned from his French embassy he too was asked for advice. At Hampton Court the King showed him the text of Leviticus and told him that he believed the marriage with Catherine was so far against the laws of nature as to be beyond dispensation by the Church. More looked up the comments of Church Fathers upon the King's biblical text: he found them unfavourable to the royal wishes. He showed them to Henry, but expressed no opinion on the validity of the bull of dispensation: he was, he said, no canon lawyer.

Wolsey's Anglo-French-Papal alliance collapsed shortly after, on the defeat of the French. It was now necessary to make peace with the Emperor: a conference was called at Cambrai. But Wolsey was unable to attend: he and an Italian Cardinal had been appointed by the Pope to try Henry and Catherine's divorce case in London. In his stead, More and Tunstall were sent to the peace conference. It was More's last diplomatic mission, and the only one in which he took enough pride to record it on his epitaph. The peace that was made lasted fourteen years, and was still in force at the time of his death.

On their return More and Tunstall found that the divorce proceedings had been interrupted by an appeal from Queen Catherine to the Pope. More had hopes that he would not be troubled further about the matter. He turned to the less disagreeable task of combating the increasing force of heresy.

4 A defender of the faith

In the year in which Thomas More joined the King's Council, a Professor of Theology at Wittenberg, Martin Luther, threw down a challenge to the Pope's pretensions that was to lead half Europe to reject Papal authority. The occasion of his protest was the proclamation of an indulgence in return for contributions to the building of the great new church of St. Peter's in Rome. The offer of an indulgence – that is, of remission of punishment due to sin – was and is a normal part of Roman Catholic practice; but this particular indulgence was promoted in such an irregular and catchpenny manner as to be a scandal even by the lax Catholic standards of the period. But Luther's attack on Catholic practices soon went much further than indulgences. By 1520 he had questioned the status of four of the Church's seven sacraments, arguing that only baptism, eucharist, and penance were authorised in the Gospels. In his book *The Liberty of the Christian Man* he stated his cardinal doctrine that the one thing needful for the justification of the sinner is faith, or trust in the merits of Christ; without this faith nothing avails, with it everything is possible.

Henry VIII viewed Luther's writings with horror, and his officials burned several of his books at St. Paul's Cross. Aided no doubt by a number of English scholars, the King published an *Assertion of the Seven Sacraments* in confutation of Lutheran doctrine. More was among those who assisted, though only, by his own account, in a minor editorial capacity. The book took a very exalted view of the authority of the Pope, and More felt it necessary to utter a word of caution.

'I must put your Highness in remembrance of one thing, and that is this. The Pope, as Your Grace knoweth, is a Prince as you are, and in league with all the other Christian Princes. It may hereafter so fall out that Your Grace and he may vary upon some points of the league, whereupon may grow breach of amity and war between you both. I think it best, therefore, that that place be amended, and his authority more slenderly touched.'

'Nay,' quoth His Grace, 'that shall it not. We are so much bounden unto the See of Rome that we cannot do too much honour to it.' (R 34)

Certainly, Pope Leo X was highly pleased by the book. In gratitude he designated Henry *Fidei Defensor* ('Defender of the Faith') : a title which is still borne on the coins of Henry's successors.

Martin Luther replied in a contemptuous and vituperative pamphlet. To reply in person would have been beneath Henry's dignity, and More was commissioned to write a riposte under an alias. More couched his reply in verbose and truculent Latin; it is only slightly better mannered than Luther's. The tone of the work at its worst can be illustrated from the following sample, in which Sister Scholastica Mandeville's translation has well preserved the flavour of the original.

Since he has written that he already has a prior right to bespatter and besmirch the royal crown with shit, will we not have the posterior right to proclaim the beshitted tongue of this practitioner of posterioristics most fit to lick with his anterior the very posterior of a pissing she-mule until he shall have learned more correctly to infer posterior conclusions from prior premises? (Y 5.123)

Erasmus, like More, was prevailed upon to write in the defence of the traditional teaching: his work *On Free Will* attacked Luther's claim that man of himself is not free to choose between good and evil. Luther replied with a substantial treatise, *On the Bondage of the Will*. More wrote a Latin letter in 1526 on similar topics in reply to a Lutheran pamphleteer's *Letter to the English*.

Lutheran ideas began to find favour in some quarters in England. None knew this better than More, for his son-in-law Roper, as we learn from Harpsfield, was one of the first to follow the new fashion. Reading Luther's works convinced him 'that faith only did justify, that the works of man did nothing profit, and that, if man could once believe that our Saviour Christ shed his precious blood and died on the cross for our sins, the same only belief should be sufficient for our salvation'. He began to think that all the ceremonies and sacraments used by the Church were vain. Such was his enthusiasm for heresy, we are told, that 'neither was he content to whisper it in hugger-mugger, but thirsted very sore to publish his new doctrine and divulge it, and thought himself very able to do so, and it were even at Paul's Cross' (H 100).

More argued with Roper, but in vain; he told Margaret,

> 'Meg, I have borne a long time with thy husband; I have reasoned and argued with him in those points of religion, and still given to him my poor fatherly counsel, but I perceive none of all this able to call him home, and therefore, Meg, I will no longer argue and dispute with him, but will clear give him over, and get me another while to God and pray for him.' (H 102)

Lutheran books were imported to London by traders from overseas; More, in 1526, ordered a search for heretical works in the German quarter. Four merchants, as a result of this search, were forced to abjure their errors at St. Paul's Cross. Roper was cautioned along with them; then or later he returned to Catholic belief.

One of the most energetic English admirers of Luther was William Tyndale, who in 1526 completed an English version of the New Testament and wrote a heretical pamphlet with the title *The Obedience of a Christian Man*. Tunstall, now Bishop of London, tried to prevent the circulation of this New Testament in his diocese; he regarded the translation as tendentious, and there was no mistaking the anti-Catholic and anti-Papal nature of some of the notes. The Bishop tried to buy up copies for destruction, but this, of course, financed further printings. More sagely, Tunstall invited More to write against Luther and Tyndale in English, so that arguments for the traditional doctrines could be read not only by scholars but by the public, who were eager readers of the new vernacular testament.

The first outcome of this was *A Dialogue concerning Heresies*, which was printed in 1529 and, slightly revised, in 1531. As it is the best written of More's anti-heretical works, we may give it consideration as a fair sample of the whole. It is cast in the form of a dialogue in the garden at Chelsea between More and a messenger sent to him by a 'right worshipful' friend to report how ignorant people are calling in doubt traditional doctrines, and murmuring about the clergy's suppression of heretics. The dialogue considers in particular the heretics' allegations that the worship of images is idolatrous, and that prayer and pilgrimages to saints are vain. It contains an interesting defence by More of vernacular versions of the Bible (which were suspect to many conservative churchmen). The fourth book may be considered in detail as a sample of the work.

At the opening of the fourth book the messenger voices the opinion that the only reason the clergy ban Luther's books is that 'they are afraid that in them laymen may read the priests' faults'. More will have none of this.

If it were now doubtful and ambiguous whether the church of Christ were in the right rule of doctrine or not, then were it very necessary to give them all good audience that could and would anything dispute on either part for or against it, to the end that, if we were now in a wrong way, we might leave it and walk in some better. But now on the other side, if it so be (as indeed it is) that Christ's church hath the true doctrine already, and the selfsame that St. Paul would not give an angel of heaven audience to the contrary, what wisdom were it now therein to shew ourself so mistrustful and wavering that for to search, whether our faith were false or true, we should give hearing, not to an angel of heaven, but to a fond friar, to an apostate, to an open incestuous lecher, a plain limb of the devil, and a manifest messenger of hell? (W 2.255)

Rebuking sinful clergy is not enough to get a book banned: the writings of many holy fathers of the past are full of such stuff. It is enough to rehearse Luther's doctrines to see that they are abominable heresies. 'He began with pardons and with the Pope's power, denying, finally, any of both to be of any effect at all. And soon after, to show what good spirit moved him, he denied all the seven sacraments, except baptism, penance and the sacrament of the altar, saying plainly that all the remnant be but fained things, and of none effect' (W 2.257). Even those sacraments he retains, Luther handles ill. The value of baptism is degraded by the doctrine that faith is all-sufficient. In the eucharist, Luther teaches, against the Catholic doctrine of transubstantiation, that bread and wine remain in the sacrament of the altar joined with the body and blood of Christ. In penance, he removed the need for a priest; every man and woman can hear confession and absolve. 'Marry,' says the messenger, 'this were an easy way.' He dislikes most confessors at sight; 'but if I might, after Luther's way, be confessed to a fair woman, I would not let to be confessed weekly' (W 2.257). More itemises Luther's 'other wild heresies':

He teacheth against scripture and all reason, that no Christian man is or can be bounden by any law made among men, nor is not bounden to observe or keep any. Item, he teacheth that there is no purgatory. Item, that all men's souls lie still and sleep till the day of doom. Item, that no man should pray to saints nor set by any holy relics nor pilgrimage, nor do any reverence to any images. (W 2.261)

Item, he teacheth that no man hath no free will, nor can anything do therewith, not though the help of grace be joined thereunto; but that everything that we do, good and bad, we do nothing at all there in ourself, but only suffer God to do all thing in us, good and bad, as wax is wrought into an image or a candle by the man's hand without anything doing thereto itself. (W 2.260)

More, in his *Dialogue*, does not offer many theological arguments against Luther's doctrine. Rather, he attacks the motives and conduct of Luther and his disciples. Luther looks at the Church 'through a pair of evil spectacles of ire and envy'; he is goaded by the 'itch and tickling of vanity and vainglory' which 'cast him clean beside his mind and memory' (W2. 267–9). He is forever inconsistent, at one moment appealing to a general council and at another utterly rejecting conciliar authority; at one time saying that no man nor angel is able to dispense with a vow made to God, and at another that no vow could bind any man at all. 'But it well appeareth that he wrote the first of anger and malice toward the pope, and then changed to the second of a lecherous lust to the nun that he minded to marry' (W 2.270).

If Luther's doctrines are suspect because of his base motives, they are manifested as wicked by their effects. Look at the Peasants' War and the massacres in its train! Look what happened

when Lutheran soldiers in the service of Charles V captured
Rome in 1527! More tells the horrors of the sack, the robberies,
mutilations, rapes and murders, and as a climax tells how

> Some failed not to take a child and bind it to a spit and lay it to
> the fire to roast, the father and mother looking on. And then
> began to bargain of a price for the sparing of the child, after
> first an hundred ducats, then fifty, then forty, then twenty,
> then ten, then five, then twain, when the poor father had not
> one left but these tyrants had all already. Then would they let
> the child roast to death. And yet in derision, as though they
> pitied the child, they would say to the father and mother,
> 'Ah, fie, fie for shame, what a marvel is it though God send a
> vengeance on you. What unnatural people be you that can
> find in your hearts to see your own child roasted afore your
> face, rather than ye would out with one ducat to deliver it
> from death.' (W 2.275)

To be sure, there are cruel and wicked men in every sect. But
other Christian men's cruelty cannot be attributed to their
Christianity, since their evil living is contrary to the doctrine of
Christ. The wickedness of Lutherans, however, arises directly
from Luther's teaching.

> For what good deed shall he study or labour to do that
> believeth Luther that he hath no free will of his own by which
> he can, with help of grace, either work or pray? Shall he not
> say to himself that he may sit still and let God alone? What
> harm shall they care to forbear, that believe Luther, that God
> alone without their will worketh all the mischief that they do
> themself? (W 2.276)

It is by licensing voluptuous living and violence that Luther
makes converts: a license symbolised by his own marriage with a
nun. What shame, 'to see such a rabble spring up among us, as

professing the faith and religion of Christ, let not to set at nought all the doctors of Christ's church, and lean to the only authority of Friar Tuck and Maid Marion' (W 2.278).

The German Lutherans, the messenger concedes, may deserve all that More says of them. But the English Lutherans seem honest and godly men; and they explain Luther's doctrines in ways that make them seem 'not much discrepant from the true faith of Christ's church'. The doctrine of justification by faith merely means that men should put their trust in God's promises rather than take pride in their own deeds. More denies this flatly. 'When Luther saith that nothing can damn any Christian man but only lack of belief, he sheweth manifestly that we not only need no good works with our faith, but also that so we have faith, none evil works can hurt us' (W 2.289). But More is more courteous with the English Lutherans than he is with Luther, and at this point he gives a lucid, though unsympathetic, theological evaluation of the doctrine of justification by faith. He agrees with the Lutherans that our works, in themselves, are of no value to God.

> But as we see that one ounce of gold whereof ten pound weight were not of his own nature toward man worth one ounce of wheat, nor one hundred pound weight thereof, of the nature self, worth one silly sheep, is yet among men, by a price appointed and agreed, worth many whole sheep, and many a pound weight of bread: so hath it liked the liberal goodness of God to set as well our faith, as our deeds, which were else both twain of their nature right little in value, at so high a price, as none is able to buy them and pay for them but himself, because we should work them only to him, and have none other paymaster. (W 2.295)

The most abominable of all the Lutheran heresies, More says, is the belief that God predestines people to damnation, when they have no liberty to choose good: 'so that God, whose goodness is inestimable, doth damn so huge a number of people to intolerable and interminable torments only for his pleasure, and for his own deeds wrought in them only by himself'. Besides being blasphemous in itself, this doctrine takes away any motive, whether threats or promises, for striving after good.

> If we be of the chosen sort, none evil deed can damn us. And if we be of the unchosen sort, no good deed can avail us. He that thus believeth, what careth he what he doth, except for the fear of temporal laws of this world? And yet if his false faith be strong, he careth little of them also. For he shall think dying in his bed or on the gallows cometh not after his deserving but hangeth all upon destiny. (W 2.299)

But no one can hold this fatalism for long consistently.

> If free will serve for nought, and every man's deed is his destiny, why do these men complain upon any man, except they will say they do it because it is their destiny to do so? And why will they be angry with them that punish heretics, except they will say because it is their destiny to be so? For if they will hold them to their own sect, and say men do them wrong to burn them for their heresies, because it was their destiny to be heretics, they may be then well answered with their own words, as one of their sect was served in a good town in Almayn, which when he had robbed a man and was brought before the judges, he could not deny the deed, but he said that it was his destiny to do it, and therefore they might not blame him; they answered him, after his own doctrine, that if it were his destiny to steal, and that therefore they must hold him excused, then it was also their destiny to hang him, and therefore he must as well hold them excused again. (W 2.300)

The rest of the dialogue is taken up with the justification of the practice of punishing heretics. 'The fear of these outrages and mischiefs to follow upon such sects and heresies, with the proof that men have had in some countries thereof, have been the cause that princes and people have been constrained to punish heresies by terrible death, whereas else more easy ways had been taken with them' (W 2.301).

The messenger says, 'I would all the world were agreed to take all violence and compulsion away on all sides, Christian and heathen, and that no man were constrained to believe but as he could be by grace, wisdom, and good works induced, and then he that would go to God, go on in God's name, and he that will go to the devil, the devil go with him' (W 2.302).

This is correct, More says, as between Christians and non-Christians: if Christ's teaching and Mahomet's are each peacefully preached, no doubt Christianity will gain many more souls than it will lose. 'But heretics rising among ourself, and springing of ourself, be in no wise to be suffered, but to be oppressed and overwhelmed in the beginning. For by any covenant with them Christendom can nothing win' (W 2.303).

Parliament, then, did well to make an Act in King Henry IV's time for the punishment of heretics. At the first fault, if a man forswears his heresy and does penance, he is received back into favour; if he is taken in the same crime again he is excommunicated, and handed over by the clergy to the secular power. It is the lay magistrate, not the bishop, who puts to death: but 'the bishop should surely not have such pity that rather than other men should punish the heretic's body he should be allowed to infect other men's souls' (W 2.305)

To punish internal heretics is as lawful as to resist the infidel by force. But some say that the present victories of the Turks against Christendom are due to the use by Christians of violence against their enemies. This is like the reasoning of an old fool in Kent at an assembly to inquire why Sandwich haven was silted up.

Some laid the fault to Goodwin Sands, others to the lands inned [enclosed] by divers owners in the Isle of Thanet. Then started up one good old father, and said he knew the cause well enough, for he had marked it going on and getting worse. 'And what hath hurt it good father?', quoth the gentlemen. 'By my faith, masters,' quod he, 'yonder same Tenterden steeple, and nothing else, that, by the mass, cholde twere a fair fish pole.' 'Why hath the steeple hurt the haven, good father?', quod they. 'Nay, by our Lady masters,' quod he, 'I cannot tell you why, but chote well it hath. For, by God, I knew it a good haven till that steeple was builded, and by the Mary mass that marked it well, it never throve since.' (W 2.307)

Bishops and magistrates could lawfully use much stricter means than they do to chastise heretics.

Surely as the princes be bounded that they shall not suffer their people by infidels to be invaded, so be they as deeply bounded that they shall not suffer their people to be seduced and corrupted by heretics, since the peril shall in short while grow to be as great, both with men's souls withdrawn to God, and their goods lost, and their bodies; destroyed by common sedition, insurrection and open war within the bowels of their own land. (W 2.309)

More ends the *Dialogue* with a prayer that God will

send these seditious sects the grace to cease, and the favourers of these factions the grace to amend, and us the grace that stopping our ears from the false enchantments of all these heretics we may, by the very faith of Christ's catholic church, so walk with charity in the way of good works in this wretched world, that we may be partners of the heavenly bliss. (W 2.324)

In answer to More's dialogue, Tyndale wrote a treatise of about ninety thousand words, printed in Antwerp in 1530. More replied in the massive *Confutacyon of Tyndales answere* – some half a million words, published as a serial: three books in 1532, five books in 1533, and a ninth volume left unfinished at his death. None but the most scholarly admirer of More could derive any pleasure or profit from reading through these increasingly crabbed polemics.

It was not only with his pen that More fought for orthodoxy: as a judge he was active in enforcing the laws against heresy, especially when he later became Lord Chancellor. During his Chancellorship six heretics were executed. Not a large number, say some of his apologists; but then, in Wolsey's much longer Chancellorship, none were executed at all. More was personally involved in detecting three of these six cases. He would not have thanked those modern biographers who have sought to play down his zeal against heresy. In answer to an anti-clerical pamphlet entitled 'A Treatise concerning the Division between the Spirituality and the Temporality', More wrote an *Apologye* in which he defended his record. He could show that there had been nothing irregular in his treatment of heretics: no brutality or cruelty in their examination; no injustice in the verdicts or sentences which had eventually been given on them. But of his part in the enforcement of the law he was not ashamed, but proud. He regarded heresy in the same way as a modern liberal magistrate regards racist propaganda: something disgusting and corrupting in itself, likely to lead to civil discord and violence, and therefore needing to be firmly stamped out. When he came to write his epitaph More described himself as a judge 'relentless towards thieves, murderers, and heretics'.

5 The troubles of the Chancellor

— around chancellorship [handwritten annotation]

The Peace of Cambrai in 1527, which was so greatly welcomed by More, was a humiliation for Henry, who had hoped for a glorious victory over the Emperor. For this, and for the slow progress of his divorce, he blamed Wolsey. Suddenly he stripped the Cardinal of the office of Chancellor and most of his rich possessions. He charged him with an offence under the old statute called *Praemunire* which forbade the acceptance of Papal appointments: this although Wolsey's power as Papal Legate had been conferred at the King's own request. Many were glad to see Wolsey fall but the Council did not find it easy to elect an acceptable successor to the Chancellorship: after long discussion the choice fell on More. The appointment was in several ways a surprising one. Neither before nor after his appointment did More exhibit or show any wish to acquire the arts by which political power is exercised; and he was the first layman to hold the Chancellorship since men could remember. Still, he had a long experience of the law which would enable him to preside in the Courts of Chancery without exasperating the courts of common law in which his own career had hitherto lain. On accepting the Chancellorship, More received an assurance from the King that he would not be expected to take any part against his conscience in proceedings about the 'great matter of the divorce'.

One of More's duties as Chancellor was to preside, commoner though he was, over the House of Lords. In November 1529 the Parliament met that was to go down in history as 'the Reformation Parliament'. More's speech at its inception was

62

a bitter attack on Wolsey, a 'great wether' among the King's flock of sheep who 'so craftily, so scabbedly, yea, and so untruly juggled with the King' that the good shepherd Henry had been forced to separate him from the sheep and give him his just deserts.

Partly because of his detachment from the divorce proceedings, More as Chancellor did not succeed to Wolsey's enormous political power. That went rather to the bluff and haughty Duke of Norfolk and the shrewd and unscrupulous Secretary, Thomas Cromwell. It was not as a politician, but as a judge, that he made his mark as Lord Chancellor. In an age when a blind eye was turned if judges enriched themselves by gifts from litigants, he avoided taking anything which even malice could represent as a bribe. At a time when family partiality often affected the course of justice, he was remembered for a 'flat decree' he gave against one son-in-law, and the stiff advice he gave to another: 'I assure thee on my faith that if the parties will at my hands call for justice, then, all were it my father stood on the one side, and the Devil on the other, his cause being good, the Devil should have right' (R 21). In an age when, as in all ages, litigants were exasperated by the law's delays More was legendary for clearing away long backlogs of cases.

More carried forward the reforms which Wolsey had introduced to bring justice within the reach of the poor, and worked hard to overcome the hostility which Wolsey's innovations had aroused among the more traditional common lawyers.

More could be proud of his work in the courts: he could look only with sorrow on the laws which went through Parliament during his Chancellorship. In 1529 the Commons passed a series of bills reducing the privileges of the clergy; 'a violent heap of mischief', said Bishop Fisher in the Lords, 'whereupon will ensue the utter ruin and danger of the Christian faith'.

Meanwhile, King Henry became more and more impatient at the slow progress of his divorce. Peers and bishops were invited to sign a memorial to the Pope in its favour: neither Fisher nor More did so. Universities at home and abroad were invited to express opinions about the divorce. The King began to toy with the idea of rejecting papal jurisdiction altogether.

Wolsey died in November 1530. A few weeks later the King accused the whole clergy, as he had formerly accused Wolsey, of violating the statute of *Praemunire* by exercising jurisdiction in Church courts. The clergy in the Canterbury Convocation sued for pardon, offering to pay a fine of £100,000. But this was not enough for Henry: they must also accept him as 'only Supreme Head of the English Church'. Despite Fisher's opposition, this was eventually accepted by the clergy, but with the qualification 'as far as the law of Christ allows.'

More's position became more and more difficult. On 30 March 1531 it was his duty to present to Parliament the opinions of the universities which had been collected in favour of the King's divorce. His speech to the Commons on this occasion was reported by a witness, the chronicler Hall:

> You of this worshipful House I am sure be not so ignorant but you know well that the King our sovereign lord hath married his brother's wife, for she was both wedded and bedded with his brother Prince Arthur, and therefore you may surely say that he hath married his brother's wife, if this marriage be good or no, many clerks do doubt.

More went on to report the judgements of the universities, so that 'all men shall openly perceive that the King hath not attempted this matter of his will or pleasure, as some strangers report, but only for the discharge of his conscience and surety of the succession of his realm'.

More was a man to choose each word with care: he expressed no opinion of his own about the divorce. But even reporting the favourable opinions of others went against the grain for a man who, in private, encouraged the defenders of Queen Catherine. He begged the Duke of Norfolk to ask the King to discharge him 'of that burdensome office of the Chancellorship, wherein, for certain infirmities of his body, he announced himself unable to serve' (R 26).

The infirmities of the body were real enough: but before release from office More was made to swallow further toads. In March 1532 the Commons presented a Supplication setting out their grievances against the clergy. In May the King demanded that all future clerical legislation in Convocation should receive the royal assent. When the bishops resisted this the King exploded. 'We thought the clergy of our realm had been our subjects wholly, but now we have well perceived they be but half our subjects, yea, and scarce our subjects: for all the Prelates at their consecration make an oath to the Pope clean contrary to the oath they make to us.' On 15 May Convocation abandoned its resistance, and yielded to all the King's demands. On the following day Thomas More gave up the Great Seal to the King.

On giving up the Chancellorship, More lost most of his income. He explained to his family that he could no longer maintain his household, and retrenchment would be necessary:

'I have been brought up', quoth he, 'at Oxford, at an Inn of Chancery, at Lincoln's Inn, and also in the King's Court, and so forth from the lowest degree to the highest, and yet have I in yearly revenue at this present little above an

hundred pounds by the year, so that now must we hereafter, if we like to live together, be contented to become
contributaries together. But, by my counsel, it shall not be
best for us to fall to the lowest fare first; we will not therefore
descend to Oxford fare, nor to the fare of New Inn, but we
will begin with Lincoln's Inn diet, where many right worshipful and of good years do live full well; which, if we find
not ourselves the first year able to maintain, then will
we next year go one step down to New Inn fare, wherewith
many an honest man is well contented. If that exceed our
ability too, then will we the next year after descend to
Oxford fare, where many grave, learned and ancient fathers
be continually conversant; which, if our power stretch not
to maintain neither, then may we yet, with bags and wallets,
go a-begging together and hoping that for pity some good
folk will give us their charity.' (R 27)

More was forced to pay off his staff: he found places for most of
them with other bishops and noblemen, and he passed on his
eight watermen, with his official barge, to Thomas Audley,
who succeeded him as Lord Chancellor. His family, and particularly his wife, found it hard to adjust to the diminished
state. But he had long warned them, 'We may not look at our
pleasure to go to heaven in feather-beds; it is not the way'
(R 95). For himself, office lost was leisure gained. 'I have
longed', he wrote to Erasmus, 'that I might have some time to
devote to God and myself, and that, by the grace of a great and
good God, and by the favour of an indulgent prince, I have at
last obtained' (L 173).

The indulgent prince, however, was unwilling to leave
More at peace. It irked him that his most honest and most
famous councillor should be at odds with him upon his great
matter. Henry married Ann Boleyn in January 1533; the
marriage was made public four months later when the new

Archbishop of Canterbury, Thomas Cranmer, annulled the marriage with Catherine. King and Archbishop had tired of waiting for the Pope's verdict: it was not until March 1534 that Pope Clement declared Catherine's marriage valid, seven years after the issue had first been raised. The Pope did not take so long to declare void the marriage with Ann and to excommunicate Henry.

In June 1533 Ann was to be crowned in Westminster Abbey. Tunstall and two other episcopal friends of More urged him to attend the coronation, and sent him twenty pounds to buy a new gown to do so. More accepted the twenty pounds but declined the invitation to the coronation. 'My lords,' he said, 'you required two things of me, the one whereof, since I was so well content to grant you, the other therefore I thought I might be the bolder to deny you.' Roper puts in his mouth a story of a Roman emperor who prescribed that the penalty for a certain offence should be death, unless the offender were a virgin. Unfortunately, the first offender was a virgin, which cast the Emperor's council into great perplexity. They were relieved of their doubt by a good plain man who said, 'Why make so much ado, my lords, about so small a matter? Let her first be deflowered and then after may she be devoured.' So too, More implied, the bishops might be deflowered by countenancing the King's new marriage; 'and when they have deflowered you, then will they not fail soon after to devour you' (R 29).

From the moment when More absented himself from Queen Ann's coronation, his friends believed, she and her friends began to seek to devour him. Her father, the Earl of Wiltshire, accused him of taking bribes while Lord Chancellor. More dealt with the accusations case by case. He had indeed been given a gilt cup by the wife of the successful litigant in *Vaughan* v. *Parnell*. But having filled it with wine, and drunk her health, he had handed it back as a New Year's gift to her husband. Another cup he had accepted from a litigant, but given a more precious one in return. The accusations of bribery all fell flat. But the affair of the Maid of Kent was a more serious matter.

Elizabeth Barton was a maidservant who began to believe, in 1525, that she was in receipt of divine visions and messages. Word of her mystical experiences reached the King. More told him that there was nothing in her utterances other than 'a right simple woman might, in my mind, speak it of her own wit well enough'. But the nun began to speak against the King's plans for marriage: if he married anyone other than Queen Catherine, one month later he would cease to rule, and die a villain's death. By the spring of 1533 the prophecy had already been falsified: in the summer she was arrested and questioned and confessed to a degree of fraudulence. Under interrogation she mentioned, among her supporters, Bishop Fisher and Thomas More. In fact, More had behaved with impeccable discretion, as he made clear in letters to Cromwell and the King: he had been careful, in conversation with her, to avoid any discussion of the King's matters, and he had indeed written to her urging her to keep from talking with any persons, specially with lay persons, 'of any such manner of things as pertain to princes' affairs or the state of the realm'. This did not prevent his name from being included, with that of the nun, her friends and John Fisher, in a Bill of Attainder brought before Parliament in February 1534. More wrote to Henry in March, reminding him that he had cleared himself, in his letter to Cromwell, of all untoward dealings with 'the wicked woman of Canterbury'.

> Our Lord for his mercy send you I should once meet with your Grace again in heaven, and there be merry with you, where among mine other pleasures this should yet be one,

that your Grace should surely see there then that (howsoever you take me) I am your true beadman now and ever have been, and will be till I die, howsoever your pleasure be to do by me. (L 203)

It was More's last letter to the King.

When the Bill came to the House of Lords, the peers insisted that More be given a chance to defend himself. He was invited before a commission of Cranmer, Audley, Norfolk and Cromwell. No word was said about the Maid of Kent. Instead, he was invited 'to add his consent' to the King's marriage to that of Parliament, bishops and universities. More replied: 'I verily hoped that I should never have heard of this matter more, considering that I have, from time to time, always from the beginning, so plainly and truly declared my mind unto His Grace, which His Highness to me ever seemed, like a most gracious Prince, very well to accept, never minding, as he said, to molest me more therewith.' They taunted him with the part he had played in the King's response to Luther, alleging that he had incited the King to overvalue the Papal power. More, who knew the exact opposite to be the truth, replied: 'These are threats for children.'

As he went home, Roper tells us, 'by the way he was very merry'. ' "Are you then put out of the Parliament Bill?", said I. "By my troth, son Roper," quoth he, "I never remembered it." ' The reason he was merry was that, as he said, 'I had given the devil a foul fall, and that with those lords I had gone so far as without shame I could never go back again' (R 34). But his name was in fact put out of the Act of Attainder: the King vented his anger by stopping his salary as Councillor. It was Cromwell who gave the good news to Roper that More's name had been excluded. But when Margaret told her father, he merely murmured that postponement was not the same thing as prevention.

6 'To lose one's head and have no harm'

The Parliament which met in January 1534 passed an Act to regulate the succession to the throne. It declared that the marriage between Henry and Catherine was against God's law, and was utterly void notwithstanding any licence, or dispensation. It fixed the succession on the offspring of the marriage with Queen Ann; on the eldest surviving son, if there should be one, or if not on the Princess Elizabeth. Catherine's daughter Mary was passed over.

Severe penalties were attached to the Act. Any who slandered the marriage with Queen Ann, or the heirs established, were guilty of treason, which carried the death penalty and forfeiture of all possessions. All the King's adult subjects were to take a public oath to observe and maintain 'the whole effects and contents of this present Act'. Those who refused to do so were guilty of misprision of treason, that is, treason in the second degree; the penalty was life imprisonment and confiscation of goods.

After the passing of the Act More was not left long at liberty. On the Sunday after Easter, he went with Roper to hear the sermon at St. Paul's. After Mass More went to see his adopted daughter, now living in his old home in Bucklersbury. There he was summoned to appear the next day at Lambeth palace to take the oath prescribed in the Act. He at once returned to Chelsea to take leave of his family. Roper records how he bade farewell the following day, after attending Mass.

Whereas he evermore used before at his departure from his wife and children, whom he tenderly loved, to have them

70

bring him to his boat, and there to kiss them all, and bid
them farewell, then would he suffer none of them forth of
the gate to follow him, but pulled the wicket after him, and
shut them all from him, and with an heavy heart, as by his
countenance it appeared, with me and our four servants
there took he his boat towards Lambeth. Wherein sitting
still sadly a while, at last he suddenly rounded me in the
ear, and said 'Son Roper, I thank Our Lord, the field is
won.' (R 36)

At Lambeth More found himself the only layman among a
group of clergy who had been summoned to swear the oath.
More was the first to be called before the Commissioners. He
was shown the oath, under the great seal; he asked for the text
of the Act of Succession, and read through the printed roll. He
compared the two carefully together, and then gave his
answer. As he wrote to Margaret a few days later:

> I showed unto them that my purpose was not to put any
> fault either in the act or any man that made it, or in the oath
> or any man that swore it, nor to condemn the conscience of
> any other man. But as for myself in good faith my con-
> science so moved me in the matter that, though I would not
> deny to swear to the succession, yet unto the oath that there
> was offered me I could not swear without the jeopardizing
> of my soul to perpetual damnation. (L 217)

Historians have sometimes been puzzled why, if More was
willing to swear to the succession established by the Act, he
refused to take the proffered oath. Was it the implicit rejection
of Papal authority in the Act's incidental remarks about dispensations from marriage impediments? Perhaps: but the matter is really quite simple. More was willing to swear to the
succession, because it was within the competence of Parliament to fix that upon anyone; but to swear to the invalidity of a

marriage which he was convinced was perfectly sound would be to invite God to endorse a falsehood.

The Commissioners told him that he was the first person to refuse to take the oath; they showed him the list of all the members of the Lords and Commons who had sworn at the last session of Parliament, and then they sent him out of the room in the hope that he would think better of his refusal. Through a window he watched the London clergy passing through the garden to take the oath; most were cheerful enough, slapping each other on the back and calling for beer at the Archbishop's buttery. Recalled before the Commissioners, he was asked why he was so obstinate that he not only refused to swear, but even to say what part of the oath went against his conscience.

More replied that he feared he had greatly displeased the King by refusing the oath. 'If I should open and disclose the causes why, I should further exasperate his Highness, which I would in no wise do, but rather would I abide all the danger and harm that might come toward me, than give his Highness any occasion of further displeasure.' The words were carefully chosen. By refusing the oath, More was making himself liable to imprisonment and forfeiture; to say that he refused it because he regarded the marriage with Catherine as valid would be treason in terms of the Act and would invite the death penalty. He would willingly, he offered, put the ground of his refusal in writing if the King would promise that this would not give offence nor bring him in danger of any Statute. The Commissioners replied that even letters patent from the King could not exempt him from the Act of Parliament. 'Well,' said More, 'if I may not declare the causes without peril, then to leave them undeclared is no obstinacy' (L 220).

The chief Commissioner, Archbishop Cranmer, then argued that since More had said he condemned nobody who swore, he could not regard it as a matter of certainty that it was wrong to swear. 'But then', he went on, 'you know for a certainty and a thing without doubt that you be bound to obey your sovereign lord your king.' More was taken aback to hear this argument from the Archbishop of Canterbury, and hesitated how to reply. But he insisted that he was not bound to obey the King in a matter which went against his conscience, provided that he had taken sufficient pains to see that his conscience was rightly informed. Indeed, if Cranmer's argument was conclusive, 'then we have a ready way to avoid all perplexities. For in whatsoever matters the doctors stand in great doubt the king's commandment given upon whither side he list solveth all the doubts' (L 221).

Secretary Cromwell was another of the Commissioners. He 'swore a great oath', More tells us, 'that he had liefer his own only son had lost his head than that I should thus have refused the oath. For surely the King's Highness would now conceive a great suspicion against me, and think that the matter of the nun of Canterbury was all conceived by my drift.' More's refusal was put in writing to be reported to the King. He asked it to be recorded that though he did not swear the oath, 'I never withdrew any man from it, nor never advised any to refuse it, nor never put, nor will, any scruple in any man's head, but leave every man to his own conscience. And me thinketh, in good faith, that so were it good reason that every man should leave me to mine' (L 222).

For four days More was kept in the custody of the Abbot of Westminster while the Commissioners considered whether he might be permitted to swear simply to the succession. But the King insisted on the full oath. It was tendered to him again on 17 April, and was again refused. On the same day Bishop Fisher likewise refused: he too was willing to swear to the succession, but not to 'the whole effects and contents of this present Act'.

73

More and Fisher were forthwith committed to the Tower. Roper recalls his wife's first visit to her father, after he had been a prisoner for about a month.

'I believe, Meg,' said Sir Thomas, 'that they that put me here, ween they have done me a high displeasure. But I assure thee, on my faith, my own good daughter, if it had not been for my wife and you that be my children, whom I account the chief part of my charge, I would not have failed long ere this to have closed myself in as strait a room and straiter too. I find no cause, I thank God, Meg, to reckon myself in worse case here than in my own house. For me thinketh God maketh me a wanton, and setteth me upon his lap and dandleth me.' (R 37)

One cause of grief to More in prison was that none of his family joined, or fully understood, his stand against the oath. Nor could he explain his reasons, even to them, without risking his words bringing him within the scope of the newly made treasons. Roper and Margaret took the oath, following the example of Bishop Tunstall. Margaret even wrote a letter to her father urging him to give in and take the oath. More, wounded, wrote back:

If I had not been, my dearly beloved daughter, at a firm and fast point (I trust in God's mercy) this good great while before, your lamentable letter had not a little abashed me, surely far above all other things, of which I hear divers times not a few terrible toward me. But surely they all touched me never so near, nor were so grievous unto me, as to see you, my well-beloved child, in such vehement piteous manner labour to persuade unto me, that thing wherein I have of pure necessity for respect unto mine own soul, so often given you so precise answer before. (L 224)

After this Margaret ceased trying to dissuade her father from his course. 'But we live in hope', she ended her next letter, 'that we shall shortly receive you again. I pray God heartily we may, if it be his holy will.'

Her stepmother, Dame Alice, found it difficult to keep patience with her husband. In an unforgettable passage Roper describes her first visit to the prisoner in the Tower.

'What the good year, Master More,' quoth she, 'I marvel that you, that have been always hitherto taken for so wise a man, will now so play the fool to lie here in this close, filthy prison, and be content thus to be shut up amongst mice and rats, when you might be abroad at your liberty, and with the favour and good will both of the King and his Council, if you would but do as all the Bishops and best learned of this realm have done. And seeing you have at Chelsea a right fair house, your library, your books, your gallery, your garden, your orchard and all other necessaries so handsome about you, where you might in the company of me your wife, your children and household be merry, I muse what a God's name you mean here still thus fondly to tarry.'

After he had a while quietly heard her, with a cheerful countenance he said unto her, 'I pray thee, good Mistress Alice, tell me one thing.'

'What is that?', quoth she.

'Is not this house', quoth he, 'as nigh heaven as my own?'

To whom she, after her accustomed homely fashion, not liking such talk, answered 'Tilly-vally, tilly-vally'.

'How say you, Mistress Alice,' quoth he, 'is it not so?'

'*Bone deus, bone deus*, man, will this gear never be left?', quoth she.

'Well then, Mistress Alice, if it be so,' quoth he, 'it is very well. For I see no great cause why I should much joy either of my gay house or of anything belonging thereunto, when, if I should but seven years lie buried under the ground, and then arise and come thither again, I should not fail to find some therein that would bid me get out of doors, and tell me it were none of mine. What cause have I then to like such an house as would so soon forget his master?' (R 41)

While in the Tower More wrote the most popular of all his devotional works, the *Dialogue of Comfort against Tribulation*. It is an imaginary conversation between two Hungarians, Antony and his nephew Vincent, about the threat of martyrdom arising from the advance of the Turk Suleiman the Magnificent into Hungary. It is a meditation on the prospect of painful death, filled with biblical allusions and drawing on Catholic doctrine for topics of comfort. It is written in a much simpler and homelier style than the works of controversy. Thus, meditating on Christ's tears over Jerusalem, More writes:

> We may see with how tender affection God in his great goodness longeth to gather under the protection of his wings, and how often like a loving hen he clucketh home unto him, even those chickens of his that willfully walk abroad into the kite's danger, and will not come at his clucking, but ever the more he clucketh for them, the farther they go from him. (D 108)

In spite of the solemn theme of the book, it is not lacking in the 'merry tales' which adorn all More's works and illustrate his gifts as a raconteur. 'There is no tale so foolish', said More, 'but that to some purpose it may hap to serve'; and with that he starts upon the fable of the ass and the wolf that went to confession to a fox: a magnificently told story, too long to quote. Vivid domestic similes are used to point a moral: chaplains who flatter a man in power are thus rebuked:

> In such wise deal they with him as the mother doth sometime with her child, which when the little boy would not rise for her in time but lie still abed and slug, and when he is up weepeth

because he hath lain so long, fearing to be beaten at school for his late coming thither, she telleth him it is but early days, and he shall come time enough, and biddeth, 'Go, good son, I warrant thee I have sent to thy master myself. Take thy bread and butter with thee. Thou shalt not be beaten at all.' And so thus she may send him merry forth at door, that he weep not in her sight at home; she studieth not much upon the matter, though he be taken tardy and beaten when he cometh to school. (D 48)

To illustrate that some tribulations are sent by God to prevent us from falling into sin, More makes use of his gift for the concrete presentation of detail and exhibits his fondness for jingle and alliteration:

Some young lovely lady, lo, that is yet good enough, God seeth a storm coming toward her that would (if her health and fat feeding should a little longer last) strike her into some lecherous love, and instead of her old-acquainted knight, lay her abed with a new-acquainted knave. But God, loving her more tenderly than to suffer her fall into such shameful beastly sin, sendeth her in season a goodly fair fervent fever, that maketh her bones to rattle, and wasteth away her wanton flesh, and beautifieth her fair skin with the colour of the kite's claw, and maketh her look so lovely that her lover would have little lust to look upon her, and maketh her also so lusty that if her lover lay in her lap, she should so sore long to break unto him the very bottom of her stomach that she should not be able to refrain it from him, but suddenly lay it all in his neck. (D 30)

It is possible to follow More's thought as he composed the work by comparing the *Dialogue* with the letters he wrote to his family and the conversations he had with visitors during his imprisonment: the same themes and some of the illustrations occur in both. Of particular interest is a letter which Margaret

Roper wrote to her stepsister Alice Alington, describing a visit to the Tower. (The letter was included in the 1557 Edition of More's *Works*.)

Margaret told More that some suspected he was unduly influenced by the example of Bishop Fisher. He replied that he had informed his own conscience; he was unable blindly to follow the judgement of another, even of a man of the wisdom, learning and virtue of Bishop Fisher.

> 'Verily, daughter, I never intend (God being my good lord) to pin my soul at another man's back, not even the best man that I know this day living; for I know not whither he may hap to carry it. There is no man living, of whom while he liveth, I may make myself sure. Some may do for favour, and some may do for fear, and so might they carry my soul a wrong way.'

More told a story of a jury which tried a London bailiff for wrongful seizure of goods. Eleven of the jurors were northerners, who were keen to give judgement against the defendant, since the plaintiff too was a northern man. The twelfth juror, an honest man, stood out; they urged him to side with them for the sake of fellowship or good company. He asked:

> 'What will happen when we shall go hence and come before God, and he shall send you to heaven for doing according to your conscience and me to the devil for doing against mine? If I shall then say to all you again, masters, I went once for good company with you, which is the cause that I go now to hell, play you the good fellows now again with me, as I went then for good company with you, so some of you go now for good company with me: would you go?'

Similarly, More said to Margaret, if he were to swear the oath out of good fellowship with his old companions, what should he say when he stands in judgement at the bar before the divine Judge?

'If he judge them to heaven and me to the devil, because I did as they did, not thinking as they thought, if I should then say, "Mine old good lords and friends, naming such a lord and such, yea and some bishops peradventure of such as I love best, I sware because you sware, and went that way that you went, do likewise for me now, let me not go alone, if there be any fellowship with you, some of you come with me."'

More doubted that he would find one who would be willing for good fellowship to go to the devil with him.

Margaret replied that she was not asking him to swear for good fellowship, but to be swayed by the authority of learned men and the commandment of Parliament. More answered:

'As for the law of the land, though every man being born and inhabiting therein, is bound to the keeping in every case upon such temporal pain, and in many cases upon pain of God's displeasure too, yet is there no man bound to swear that every law is well made, nor bound upon the pain of God's displeasure to perform any such point of the law as were indeed unlawful. Of which manner kind, that there may such hap to be made in any part of Christendom, I suppose no man doubteth, the General Council of the whole body of Christendom excepted.'

Margaret was at her wits' end and said that she could offer no further argument, except the one made by Henry Patenson, her father's jester. He, told that More was in the Tower, had said: 'What aileth him that he will not swear? Wherefore should he stick to swear? I have sworn the oath myself.' So Margaret, after offering in vain the example of so many wise men, could only say, 'Why should you refuse to swear, father, for I have sworn myself?' At this More laughed and said, 'That word was like Eve too, for she offered Adam no worse fruit than she had eaten herself.'

Before leaving, Margaret passed on to More a warning she had received from Cromwell. 'Master Secretary sent you word as your very friend, to remember, that Parliament lasteth yet.' Further legislation might bring More yet again within danger of the death penalty. More replied that he had long considered this possibility: but no law could be made which could justly bring him into further danger, and in such a case 'a man may lose his head and have no harm'.

The seventh session of the Reformation Parliament opened in November 1534. More had now been imprisoned for seven months and had still not been brought to trial. He could have been charged with misprision of treason for refusing to take the oath to the Succession Act, and it is uncertain why proceedings were not brought. More himself told Margaret that his detention was irregular because the oath administered to him was of a form not specified in the Statute. If this was the defect, it was to be remedied in the new session of Parliament.

Four Acts of this session affected More's fate. The first was the Act of Supremacy, which declared that the King was supreme head of the English Church, and rejected all foreign authority in ecclesiastical matters. A second Act of Succession regularised the oath which had been exacted under the previous Act. A new Act of Treasons was passed which made it treasonous to attempt to deprive the King of any of his titles, including the title conferred by the Act of Supremacy. To be guilty of treason in this way it was not necessary to proceed from words to deeds: it was enough if a person did 'maliciously wish, will, or desire, by words or writing,' so to do. Finally, at the end of the session, Acts of Attainder were passed against More, Fisher and five other non-juring clergy.

The Act of Attainder denounced More for his obstinate

refusal to take the oath: it condemned him, without the need for further trial, to imprisonment for life, and confiscation of goods. But the new treason act went further: it would bring him to the scaffold if he was ever incautious enough to deny the Royal Supremacy before witnesses. Four months after the Parliament was prorogued, on 30 April 1535, More was interrogated in the Tower by Cromwell and other members of the Council, including the Solicitor-General, Sir Richard Rich. More described the scene a few days later in a letter to Margaret.

Cromwell asked whether he had seen the new Statutes. More said that he had, but that he had looked only briefly at the book and had not studied their effect. Had he not then read the first, of the King being Head of the Church? The members of the Council present had been instructed by the King to ask his opinion of it. More answered that the King well knew his mind on the matter. 'I neither will dispute King's title nor Pope's, but the King's true faithful subject I am and will be, and daily pray for him and all his, and for you all that are of his honourable Council, and for all the realm, and otherwise than this I never intend to meddle.' Cromwell told him that this manner of answer would not content the King. Even though a life prisoner, he was still bound to obey the Statutes, and the King would let the laws take their course against those who were obstinate. More replied, 'I do nobody harm, I say none harm, I think none harm, but wish everybody good. If this be not enough to keep a man alive in good faith, I long not to live.' Two days before, as More knew, a group of Carthusians had been condemned to be hanged, drawn and quartered for denying the Supremacy. On Margaret's next visit, on 4 May, he watched with her as the three set off on the way to Tyburn to be executed. The sight did not weaken his resolution: he expressed only envy of the priests going cheerfully to the vision of God.

King Henry played cat and mouse with him. A few days later Cromwell brought him a comforting message: the King, he reported, had decided to trouble his conscience no further. More was not deceived; when Cromwell departed he wrote with a piece of charcoal the following verses:

> Eye-flattering fortune, look thou never so fair
> Nor never so pleasantly begin to smile
> As though thou wouldst my ruin all repair,
> During my life thou shalt not me beguile.
> Trust I shall God, to enter, in a while,
> His haven of heaven, sure and uniform;
> Ever after thy calm look I for a storm.

The storm came when news reached England that the Pope had made Bishop Fisher a Cardinal. The King was enraged. 'Let the Pope send him a hat when he will,' he raged; 'I will so provide that whenever it cometh he shall wear it on his shoulders, for head shall he have none to set it on.' The Council redoubled their efforts to trap More and Fisher into an explicit denial of the Supremacy.

On 3 June Audley, Cranmer and Cromwell examined More again in the Tower. The King commanded him, Cromwell reported, to make a plain answer whether the statute was lawful, and either to acknowledge the King as Supreme Head or else 'to utter plainly his malignity'. More replied that he had no malignity to utter: he was a loyal servant of the King. 'I have always from the beginning truly used myself to looking first upon God and next upon the King according to the lesson that His Highness taught me at my first coming to his noble service, the most virtuous lesson that ever prince taught his servant.' It was hard to be compelled to make a plain answer. 'For if it were so that my conscience gave me against the statutes (wherein how my mind giveth me I make no declaration), then I nothing doing nor nothing saying against the statute it were a very hard thing to compel me to say either precisely with it against my conscience to the loss of my soul, or precisely against it to the destruction of my body.'

Cromwell asked if More had not examined heretics, when Lord Chancellor, and compelled them to answer precisely whether they believed the Pope to be head of the Church? There was a difference between the cases, More replied, 'because at that time as well here as elsewhere through the corps of Christendom the Pope's power was recognised for an undoubted thing which seemeth not like a thing agreed in this realm, and the contrary taken for truth in other realms'.

'They were as well burned for the denying of that as they be beheaded for denying of this,' said Cromwell, 'and therefore as good reason to compel them to make precise answer to the one as to the other.' The difference that mattered, More insisted, was the difference between a conscience which conflicted with a local law, and one which conflicted with a law 'of the whole corps of Christendom'. 'The reasonableness or the unreasonableness in binding a man to precise answer standeth not in the difference between beheading or burning, but because of the difference in charge of conscience, the difference standeth between beheading and hell.'

The commissioners failed to trap the prisoner into any direct denial of the Supremacy. As he was dismissed More was asked why, if he was, as he said, ready to die, did he not speak out plain against the statute? The reply was characteristic of him. 'I have not been a man of such holy living as I might be bold to offer myself to death, lest God for my presumption might suffer me to fall.'

Servants in the Tower were interrogated about letters which had passed between Fisher and More. Each had naturally been anxious to know how the other was faring: but nothing in the correspondence could be made out to be a conspiracy to deny the Supremacy. Fisher had argued that since the Statute made it an offence only to deny the royal title 'maliciously', a man would be safe from its penalties if he spoke nothing in malice. More replied that he feared that the statute would not be so interpreted.

The conditions of More's imprisonment had been, up to this point, comparatively humane: he had been allowed to employ a servant and to keep papers and books. The Council now decided to employ greater rigour. Two servants of Cromwell were sent to remove his books; with them came Sir Richard Rich. Unknown to More, a few days earlier Rich had succeeded, by pretending to seek confidential advice, in entrapping Fisher into an explicit denial of the Supremacy. He clearly hoped to do the like with More. After a flattering allusion to More's legal learning, he put to him a case.

'Admit there were, Sir, an Act of Parliament that all the Realm should take me for King. Would not you, Master More, take me for King?

'Yes, sir,' quoth Sir Thomas More, 'that would I.'

'I put case further', quoth Master Rich, 'that there were an Act of Parliament that all the Realm should take me for Pope. Would not you then, Master More, take me for Pope?'

More gave no direct reply; instead he put another case in turn. 'Suppose the Parliament would make a law that God should not be God. Would you then, Master Rich, say that God were not God?' 'No Parliament, replied Rich, 'may make any such law.' More, in silence, left the moral to be drawn, and Rich departed saying, 'Well, Sir, God comfort you, for I see your mind will not change, which I fear will be very dangerous for you.'

This visit did indeed prove dangerous: it was decided to make the exchange with Rich the basis of an indictment. Fisher was tried and convicted on 17 June and beheaded on Tower Hill five days later. On the first day of July it was More's turn to face trial in Westminster Hall.

1535

The charge in the indictment was that More had 'traitorously and maliciously, by craft imagined, invented, practised, and attempted, wholly to deprive our sovereign lord the King of his dignity, title and name of Supreme Head in earth of the Church of England'. It was based on three counts: the accused's silence at the interrogation of 7 May, his correspondence with Fisher, and his conversation with Rich.

More replied to the first count, 'Your statute cannot condemn me to death for such silence, for neither your statute nor any laws in the world punish people except for words or deeds.' The King's proctor said that silence was proof of malice. 'Surely,' replied More, 'if what the common law says is true, that he who is silent seems to consent, my silence should rather be taken as approval.'

In his correspondence with Fisher More denied that he had said, as alleged, that the statute was 'like a sword with two edges, for if a man answer one way, it will confound his soul, and if he answer the other way, it will confound his body'. He had only written conditionally: '*If* the statute cut both ways like a two-edged sword, how could a man behave so as not to incur either danger?'

Rich now gave evidence on the final count. He told the story of the exchange, and attributed to More a damning additional remark: 'No more than Parliament could make a law that God were not God could Parliament make the King Supreme Head of the Church.'

Against whom thus sworn, Sir Thomas More began in this wise to say, 'If I were a man, my lords, that did not regard an oath, I needed not, as it is well known, in this place, at this time, nor in this case, to stand here as an accused person. And if this oath of yours, Master Rich, be true, then pray I that I never see God in the face, which I would not say, were it otherwise to win the whole world.'

He then gave the true version of the conversation, and said: 'In good faith, Master Rich, I am sorrier for your perjury than for my peril.' He listed matters which undermined Rich's credit, then, turning to the bench, he said:

'Can it therefore seem likely unto your honourable lordships that I would, in so weighty a cause, so unadvisedly overshoot myself as to trust Master Rich, a man of me always reputed for one of so little truth, as your lordships have heard, so far above my sovereign lord the King, or any of his noble Councillors, that I would unto him utter the secrets of my conscience touching the King's Supremacy, the special point and only mark at my hands so long sought for, a thing which I never did, nor never would, after the statute thereof made reveal either to the King's Highness himself, or any of his honourable Councillors?'

Two witnesses were called who had been present during the exchange. Neither of them would confirm either Rich's or More's account: they had been too busy, they said, trussing More's books in a sack to give ear to the talk.

Despite the weakness of the evidence, the jury took less than a quarter of an hour to find More guilty. Lord Chancellor Audley began to pronounce sentence, but he was interrupted by the prisoner. 'My lord,' said More, 'when I was toward the law the manner in such case was to ask the prisoner before judgement, why judgement should not be given against him.' The Chancellor gave way, and More, liberated by the verdict

86

from his long silence, at last spoke his mind about the Act of Supremacy:

'Seeing that I see ye are determined to condemn me (God knoweth how) I will now in discharge of my conscience speak my mind plain and freely touching my Indictment and your Statute withal. And forasmuch as this Indictment is grounded upon an Act of Parliament directly repugnant to the laws of God and his Holy Church, the supreme Government of which, or of any part whereof, may no temporal Prince presume by any law to take upon him, as rightfully belonging to the See of Rome, a spiritual pre-eminence by the mouth of our Saviour himself, personally present upon earth, only to St. Peter and his successors, Bishops of the same See, by special prerogative granted; it is therefore in law, amongst Christian men, insufficient to charge any Christian man.'

The English Parliament could no more make a law against the law of the Universal Church than the City of London could make a law against an Act of Parliament. The Supremacy Act was contrary to the very first article of Magna Charta and to the coronation oath to uphold the rights of the Church.

The Lord Chancellor reminded More that the universities, the bishops and all the most learned men in the kingdom had agreed to the Act. More replied:

'If the number of Bishops and Universities be so material as your Lordship seemeth to take it then I see little cause, my lord, why that thing in my conscience should make any change. For I nothing doubt but that, though not in this Realm, yet in Christendom about, of these well learned Bishops and virtuous men that are yet alive, they be not the fewer part that be of my mind therein. But if I should speak of those which already be dead, of whom many be now Holy

Saints in heaven, I am very sure it is the far greater part of them that, all the while they lived, thought in this case that way that I think now. And therefore am I not bound, my lord, to conform my conscience to the Council of one Realm against the General Council of Christendom.'

The Lord Chancellor now invited the opinion of Lord Fitz-James, the Lord Chief Justice of the King's Bench, on the sufficiency of the indictment. 'By St. Just,' he said, a little lamely, 'I must needs confess that if the Act of Parliament be not unlawful, then is not the Indictment in my conscience insufficient.' Whereupon the Lord Chancellor passed sentence. More was allowed a final word:

'Like the Blessed Apostle St. Paul, as we read in the Acts of the Apostles, was present, and consented to the death of St. Stephen, and kept their clothes that stoned him to death, and yet be they now both twain Holy Saints in heaven, and shall continue there friends for ever, so I verily trust and shall therefore right heartily pray, that though your lordships have now here in earth been judges to my condemnation, we may yet hereafter in heaven merrily all meet together, to our everlasting salvation.'

More was led out of Westminster Hall and taken back to the Tower. At Tower Wharf Margaret Roper was waiting.

As soon as she saw him, after his blessing on her knees reverently received, she, hasting towards him and, without consideration or care of herself, pressing in among the midst of the throng and company of the guard that with halberds and bills went round about him, hastily ran to him, and there openly in the sight of them all, embraced him, took him about the neck and kissed him. Who, well liking her most natural and daughterly affection towards him, gave her his fatherly blessing and many godly words of comfort besides.

The penalty for treason was to be hanged, drawn and quartered; the King graciously permitted More to be executed with an axe, the privilege of a peer. Four days elapsed between trial and execution. Margaret's maid visited the Tower each day; she brought back More's hair shirt and his last letter to his daughter, with keepsakes for the members of his family.

Our Lord bless you good daughter and your good husband and your little boy and all yours and all my children and all my godchildren and all our friends . . . I cumber you good Margaret much, but I would be sorry, if it should be any longer than tomorrow, for it is St. Thomas Eve and the octave of St. Peter, and therefore tomorrow long I to go to God, it were a day very meet and convenient for me. I never liked your manner toward me better than when you kissed me last for I love when daughterly love and dear charity hath no leisure to look to worldly courtesy. Farewell my dear child and pray for me, and I shall for you and all your friends that we may merrily meet in heaven.

On the day after this letter was written, Sir Thomas Pope brought word that More was to be executed before nine o'clock; the King's wish was that at his execution he should not use many words. More asked that Margaret be allowed to be present at his burial, and was told that permission had already been given for all the family to be there.

More intended to be beheaded in his best gown, but was persuaded by the Lieutenant of the Tower that cloth-of-gold would be wasted on the executioner, so he went to the scaffold in front of the Tower in his servant's coarse grey gown. 'Going up the scaffold, which was so weak that it was ready to fall, he said merrily to Master Lieutenant, "I pray you, Master Lieutenant, see me safe up, and for my coming down let me shift for myself." ' In obedience to the King's command he said little before execution, merely asking the people's prayers and protesting that he died in and for the Catholic faith. 'Afterwards, he exhorted them and earnestly beseeched them to pray God for the King, so that He would give him good counsel, protesting that he died his good servant, but God's first.'

7 The man for all seasons

Since his death Thomas More has continued to fascinate and attract later generations, and to be admired by people of different religions or of none. His influence on later ages has been less through his writings than through the story of his life. Just as Samuel Johnson is remembered less for his *Dictionary* and for his *Lives of the Poets* than for his conversation in the pages of Boswell's *Life*, so the sayings of More that have echoed in the minds of succeeding generations have not been quotations from his own works so much as the remarks, merry or sober or both at once, that have been preserved in his son-in-law's biography. Apart from *Utopia* and the *Dialogue of Comfort*, More's writings would have been quickly forgotten had it not been for the remarkable life and death of their author.

It is not easy, however, to identify precisely the source of More's appeal to the wide circle of his admirers. It is not to be wondered at, of course, that he has been admired and venerated by Roman Catholics and canonised as a saint of the Church of Rome. He was executed, after all, because he refused to consent to Acts of Parliament which negated Papal supremacy. But it would be wrong to think of him as a martyr for that exalted concept of the Papacy, typical of devout Catholics in the late nineteenth and early twentieth centuries, which found its most triumphal expression in the definition of the primacy and infallibility of the Pope at the first Vatican Council in 1870.

For the first Vatican Council the authority of the Pope was supreme over all General Councils of the Church; More never placed the Pope above Councils. The Vatican Council proclaimed that all Christians must believe that the supremacy of the Pope was directly instituted by Christ; for much of his life More believed that the Papacy was an ecclesiastical institution of gradual growth, and never ceased to regard the matter as one on which good Christians might reasonably differ. Devout Catholics at the time of First Vatican regarded the Italian dominions of the Church as essential to the Papal office: More realised very well how the temporal sovereignty of the Popes could interfere with their pastoral mission. In recent decades it has been characteristic of loyal Catholics to admire and venerate not only the office but the person of a Pope; More, living in the most worldly period of the Vatican's history, writes of the Pontiffs at best in a tone of embarrassed apologetic, at times with an irony verging on contempt. Indeed, the Popes and the Papacy are mentioned astonishingly rarely in his voluminous anti-Protestant writings. It has been well said that if More had been told in advance that he was to die a Christian martyr, and had been told that he could die for the doctrine of his choice, the Supremacy of the Pope would have been the very last article of faith which he would have selected.

Yet, in the end, it was the Papal Supremacy for which he died, and not for the seven sacraments or for the traditional practices of Catholic piety which he defended with so much greater enthusiasm in his writings. And there was in this, after all, something entirely fitting. For even in its worst times the universal authority of the Papacy had been a symbol, however obscured by the local dynastic ambitions of vicious Popes, of the essential unity of Christian peoples in a single commonwealth of Christendom. And this was something about which More cared throughout his life. He entered public life in the service of Wolsey's plan for universal comity between

Christian nations: the proudest moment of his diplomatic career was his part in the Peace of Cambrai. He fought the heresy of Luther and withstood the autocracy of Henry because both worked to split the unity of the Christian commonwealth; in the Tower and at his trial his appeal was from the nationalist usurpation of the English Parliament to the supreme judgement of the larger body of Christendom.

Many who do not share More's beliefs have admired him as a prisoner and martyr of conscience. This indeed he was, but it is important not to misunderstand the operation of his conscience. More is best known to many of the present generation as the hero of Robert Bolt's play *A Man for All Seasons*. Bolt conceives More as 'a man with an adamantine sense of his own self' – a man who knew how far he would yield to love and to fear, but who became rigorous and unyielding when at last 'he was asked to retreat from that final area where he located his self'.

At many points in his play Bolt stresses More's sense of self. When Margaret urges him to take the oath of succession More says, 'When a man takes an oath he's holding his own self in his own hands. Like water; and if he opens his fingers then, he needn't hope to find himself again.' In the trial scene More tells Cromwell, 'In matters of conscience the loyal subject is more bounden to be loyal to his conscience than to any other thing.' 'And so provide a noble motive', retorts Cromwell, 'for his frivolous self-conceit!' 'It is not so, Master Cromwell – very and pure necessity for respect of my own soul.' 'Your own self, you mean!', says Cromwell. 'Yes', replies More, 'a man's soul is his self.' And a stage direction underlines the importance of this confrontation: 'They hate each other and each other's standpoint.'

Bolt's play is vividly written, accurate often in detail, and uses many of More's own words: none the less, the man it portrays is very different from the real More, who would not have agreed that a man's soul is a self of the kind described by Bolt. It is true that More said, when accused of being influenced by Fisher in refusing the oath, 'I never intend to pin my soul at another man's back.' It is true that he refused to condemn those who did take the oath. Thus he can be made to appear as a forerunner of modern ideas of toleration and respect for sincerity, and the contemporary notion that each man must make his own moral decisions for himself. In these respects his attitude seems to contrast with the intolerance and authoritarianism of the medieval Church and the Renaissance state.

Set in their context, however, More's remarks take on a different appearance. For him, as for Thomas Aquinas before him, the human conscience was not an autonomous lawgiver. Rather, a man's conscience was his belief, true or false, about the law made by God. To act against conscience was always wrong, because it was acting against what one believed to be God's law. But to act in accordance with conscience was not necessarily right; for one's conscience might be an erroneous opinion. One had a duty to inform one's conscience correctly; perhaps by consulting the Scriptures, or the writings of the Saints, or the authoritative documents of the Church. It was thus that More tried to inform his own and the King's conscience in the difficult matter of the divorce. The only case where a mistaken conscience would excuse from wrongdoing would be where the moral issue in question was a debatable one, where there was a division of opinion among the saints and sacred writers.

On this theory, it was not enough to act in accord with one's conscience: one's conscience must be rightly informed. Thus More, when he told Cranmer that it was against his conscience to swear, added: 'I have not informed my conscience either suddenly or slightly, but by long leisure and diligent search for the matter.' But for the More in Bolt's play what matters is not whether the Pope's supremacy is true, but the fact that More has committed his inmost self to it. As he says to Norfolk, 'What matters to me is not whether it's true or not, but that I believe it to be true, or rather not that I believe it, but that *I* believe it.'

The reason why More would not pin his soul to another man's back was not that each man must be his own lawgiver in morals: it was simply that no man could be trusted to persevere in correct conscience. When More refused to condemn others' consciences, it was not that he did not think their judgements were incorrect. He thought so, and said so, to both Cromwell and Henry, before ever he was imprisoned in the Tower. But he did not meddle with others' consciences, in the sense that he did not try to convert others to his way of thinking. Nor did he censure them, or set himself as judge over them: 'I will not misjudge any other man's conscience', he said, 'which lyeth in their own heart far out of my sight.' But this was because the particular matters at issue – the legitimacy of the Act of Succession and the oath thereto – were disputable matters, matters in that restricted area where a man might have an erroneous conscience without moral fault. It is quite clear that More had no general theory that conscience is a sufficient justification for action. He never suggested that Luther and Tyndale were excusable because they were acting according to their consciences in denying Catholic doctrine.

The comparison was made by Cromwell when More refused to give a precise answer about the lawfulness of the Act of Supremacy. Had not More forced heretics to answer precisely whether the Pope were Head of the Church? There was a difference between the cases, More replied: the Pope's power was recognised throughout Christendom, which was not like a matter which was agreed in England while the contrary was taken for truth in other realms. Whenever the real More appealed against the laws of England, it was never to some private soul or self within, but to 'the whole corps of Christendom' without. And what he feared to incur, by taking the oath, was not a metaphysical spilling of self, but the everlasting loss of God.

Naturally, a playwright is at liberty to adapt history to his purpose. No doubt, when so few people share More's beliefs in the damnation of perjurors or in the unique authority of the Roman Catholic Church, the hero of the play can be made more comprehensible if these beliefs are taken metaphorically and interpreted as a sense of selfhood or a concern for society's protection against the terrifying cosmos. None the less, the More of Bolt's play turns out to be a less consistent character than the real More.

In the play, it is difficult to make out the difference between the loyalty to self which is admirable in More and the obstinacy which Cromwell blames him for. The More of the play seems to combine a tender respect for his private conscience with an exaggerated deference to public law. Conscience and law, as the play represents them, seem to be irreconcilable values: conscience the expression of the individual will, and law the invention of the communal reason. Above all, it is hard to see why the More of the play sticks where he does. Why does he both refuse to take the oath and refuse to tell anyone why he refuses? Why should his conscience make him so unbending against one of the King's laws, so anxious to comply with another?

In the More of history there was no real conflict between conscience and law, for true conscience is simply the right appreciation of God's law. Human laws must be obeyed, in general, provided that they do not conflict with God's laws.

To show that the Act of Succession was a law which should not be obeyed, More did not appeal to any metaphysical self. 'If there were no one but my self upon my side, and the whole Parlement upon the other,' he said, 'I would be sore afraid,' but 'I am not bounden to change my conscience and conform it to the council of our realm against the general council of Christendom.' Yet, so far as he could, he would obey the King's law, including the law against positively speaking against the Act; for he did not wish presumptuously to expose himself to the death penalty. More's appeal against the courts of the realm of England is not to the narrow, interior, metaphysical court of his own self, but to the wider, public, universal court of the community of Christian nations.

The More of Bolt's play is not only very different from the martyr on Tower Hill: he is unrecognisable as the same person as the author of *Utopia*. The constitution of Utopia is designed, as scholars have emphasised, for the purpose of excluding Pride. This purpose governs even the economic arrangements, the absence of money and the lack of a market. Pride is the canker of the commonwealth, the peculiarly human vice which makes men more greedy than the beasts. The author of *Utopia* would surely view the hero of Bolt's play as puffed up with pride. In this point the Cromwell of the play is closer to the true More when he condemns its hero's fiendish self-conceit. A man's soul is his self, says Bolt's More. Not so, says the real More. In Utopia as in Christendom, a man's soul is never more healthy than when it is at its most selfless.

But if Bolt's More contrasts with the More of real life, is there not an equally great contrast between the Catholic martyr and the author of *Utopia*? How can we – people ask – reconcile the tolerant humanist who wrote the dialogue with the bigoted Chancellor who fought heretics with his pen and through the courts? Wherever we turn in *Utopia*, it seems, we find something which is contradicted in More's life. More has attracted admirers in every generation above all as a man of integrity. But integrity means wholeness: how can we speak of More's integrity when there seems to be a mass of inconsistencies between his life and death on the one hand and the contents of his best-known work on the other?

Let us list some of the inconsistencies which have been detected between the practices of Utopia and More's own conduct. First, the Utopians have few laws and small regard for lawyers: More devoted most of his life to the law and became England's chief law officer. Secondly, Utopians despise the precious metals, while regarding ascetic practices as a mark of folly; More, in and out of office, wore a golden chain, and beneath it a shirt of hair to tame his flesh. In Utopia, thirdly, it is lawful to follow, peaceably, any religion one chooses; More prided himself on his reputation as a severe castigator of heretics. Fourthly, in *Utopia* the clergy are allowed to marry, and indeed to select the choicest partners; More, in controversy with Luther, harps beyond the bounds of taste on his marriage with a nun as nullifying all his doctrinal claims. Fifthly, divorce is permitted in Utopia on comparatively easy terms; in life More went to prison rather than consent to a divorce which half the divines of Christendom thought was allowable according to Scripture and canon law. Sixthly, suicide in Utopia, in appropriate circumstances, is regarded as permissible and even laudable; More, however weary of life in the Tower, was scrupulously careful not to utter a word that would bring him within the death penalty and thus create a risk that he would face God before God had called him. Seventhly, the constitution of Utopia is radically egalitarian; More, right up to his death, behaved to the tyrant Henry with an obsequiousness bordering on servility which could not, as it could in the case of others less brave, be attributed to fear. Finally, in *Utopia* the Papacy is spoken of with contemptuous irony; it was, in the end, for the prerogatives of the Pope that More gave his life.

It would not be difficult to prolong such a list of paradoxes. How are they to be resolved?

Some of the contrasts we have listed are doubtless over-drawn. The Utopians regard unprofitable asceticism as perverse, but they do admire those who choose austerity in the service of others. Though they do not imprison heretics, Utopians debar from office those who hold particularly obnoxious religious beliefs. But even when the emphasis has been rectified, the conflicts remain: More's austerities went beyond those approved by the Utopians, and Tyndale's heresies were well within the bounds of Utopian toleration. The inconsistencies are still in need of reconciliation.

Some despair of reconciliation, and write off either the Catholic More or the Utopian More. Socialists have admired the anti-market communism of the early work, and regretted the gradual corruption of More into a persecuting zealot obsessed with death and an imaginary afterlife. Catholics have invited us to regard *Utopia* as a joke, or as a youthful indiscretion for which More was later to make ample amends in his sufferings for orthodoxy.

Both approaches are mistaken. One cannot make a contrast between cheerful, far-sighted humanism in More's youth and morbid bigotry in his later days. Contemporary with *Utopia* there survive meditations on death, as full of Christian pessimism about the ways of the world as anything which More wrote in the Tower. Nor can *Utopia* be dismissed as a joke. It is More's most careful piece of writing; and the constitution of the imaginary Republic is attached to a dialogue discussing a question which More took deeply seriously, the pros and cons of a humanist entering the public service. Of course it is full of wit; but More's wit is never a sign of frivolous purpose.

Utopia is undoubtedly meant seriously: but in what way are we to take it seriously? It is not intended, any more than Plato's *Republic*, as a model constitution for an actual state, such as was drawn up by the founding fathers of the United States. Nor is it meant as a description of an ideal, though unfortunately unattainable, society. The word 'Utopian' suggests to us the notion of unpractical idealism. But when More coined the word, it carried no suggestion that the constitution it referred to was ideal. If to us 'Utopian' suggests 'desirable', that is because many readers of More's work have found the conditions he describes attractive and inspiring. The treatise does indeed inquire into the best form of commonwealth; but the Utopian constitution is not presented as the simple answer to the inquiry.

To a modern, secular reader many of the provisions of the Utopian constitution seem humane and far-sighted. Not all find enticing the money-free communism and the absence of privacy; but the ideal of secular, bisexual, quasi-monastic communities sharing the fruits of their labours has been influential in our own time in capitalist no less than in socialist countries. Had the Utopian rules about colonisation and the conduct of war been adopted by Christian countries in the centuries after More's death, the world's history would have been far happier. The provisions concerning suicide, divorce and penal practice in Utopia may well seem to the reader preferable to the code enforced in Christian countries in More's time, or to the mores prevailing in Western countries in our own.

But did More himself mean the reader to find the Utopians' practices admirable? Some of them, such as the permission of divorce and suicide, went clean against Christian teaching: members of societies which tolerated such things should have been, according to the orthodox teaching, condemned or pitied rather than admired. Did More think that a society such as Utopia was even possible? According to a Christian tradition which claimed Augustine as its spokesman, human nature was so corrupt after the Fall that without grace no one could long keep the most basic precepts of the natural law. Could a society like Utopia, ignorant of Christ and out of touch with the means of grace, uphold such a rewarding life and provide an environment for so many virtues to flourish?

I believe that More did mean us to admire many things in Utopia, and that he may well have thought a society such as he described was possible, though naturally he was amused when some of his contemporaries took the work at face value as a description of an actual civilisation in a distant land. Augustinian pessimism about the possibilities of nature unaided by grace was soon to be restated and dramatically heightened by reformed theologians, and was affirmed by the Council of Trent in tones only slightly less stark. But at the time when More wrote, the Augustinian tradition was partly in eclipse, as Luther was loudly to complain. It seems possible that More combined a deep pessimism about the society in which he lived with optimism about what might have happened in societies with a different history.

One message which *Utopia* is meant to carry to the reader is clear. The Utopians are pagans, who lack the privileges of Christians who have received divine revelation through Christ and the Church. See how well they manage to behave, what peaceful and rewarding lives they live on the basis of their lesser light! We Christians, who have incomparably greater advantages, behave far worse than they do in such matters as the treatment of the poor, faithfulness to our wives, the keeping of treaties, the making of war, the exploitation of subject peoples.

This does not mean that the Utopians are better off without Christianity. Had they accepted Christianity they would have had to abandon some of their practices; to have adopted tighter rules about marriage and against euthanasia, for instance. In exchange they would have learnt many truths about man and God, and have received the promise of a more glorious immortality. Perhaps among the things they would have had to give up would have been their hardy equality, having accepted a hierarchical Church and maybe a quasi-sacramental monarchy. There is no reason, though, why they should have had to give up their familial communism; and as Christians they would have been able to appreciate better the selflessness of those who choose celibate and vegetarian lives to care for the sick and perform unpopular labour. Utopians converted to Christianity would put European Christians to shame even more than did the unconverted pagans described in the dialogue. And once converted, they would no longer find rational that toleration of error which was appropriate when they were uncertain seekers after religious truth.

The lack of an unambiguous and explicit political or theological message is, of course, part of the fascination of *Utopia*; in its ironic temper, as in other things, it resembles the *Republic* of Plato. In style and in form *Utopia* is very much a work of the Renaissance: one cannot imagine a medieval political treatise susceptible of such varied and contradictory interpretations.

Utopia indeed shows Christian humanism's most attractive face. When we turn from it to More's controversial writings we see a more repellent product of humanist education. Many of the matters which More debated with Luther and Tyndale had been subjects of controversy among scholastic theologians over several centuries. The scholastic debate had been conducted in a manner which, though it might seem arid and technical, was almost always sober and courteous. But humanist education replaced the study of formal patterns of argument with a systematic quest for rhetorical effect. The model of Latin style was Cicero, who had made his name as an attorney anxious to make the most persuasive case for his client or the most damning indictment of his opponent. Humanist scholars practised their wits, as More himself did, in the composition of diatribe and invective. It was not a training which was likely to make for fairness and moderation in controversy. More, writing against the Protestants, is always a barrister hectoring a hostile witness; he is far removed from a scholastic like Thomas Aquinas, always anxious to put the best possible interpretation on the position of those he disagrees with.

More, to be sure, was replying in kind to the invective of Luther. Both Luther and More shared a disdain for recent scholastic theology; both of them shared the humanistic desire to cut through systematic theological speculation to the closer study of the Scriptures and early Christian texts; both of them shared an enthusiasm for elaborate and rhetorical abuse on the classical model. The pugnacious conventions of humanist debate were one of a number of factors which led to the hardening of positions on each side. If More and Luther had been able and willing to bring to such issues as the doctrine of justification that patient willingness to understand rival positions which characterised scholastic debate, the theological gap between them might well have narrowed. Had they been less suspicious of the apparatus of logical distinctions developed in the Middle Ages, they might have been able to see ways of reconciling theological opinions which on the surface clashed. It was in part the scholarly climate of the Renaissance which made the Reformation so divisive.

More's polemical works are now read only by historians; *Utopia* continues to entertain and instruct. Indeed, for those who do not share More's religious premisses, *Utopia* stands out among his works much more than it has ever done for his co-religionists. But even the most secular reader of *Utopia* cannot help, as he reads the book, reminding himself constantly of its author's eventual martyrdom.

It is not fanciful to link the ideals of *Utopia* with More's final constancy. If only More's fellow Catholics can fully enter into what More died *for*, all too many people in the present age have had experience of what he died *against*. The imposition of a novel ideology by fear and force is hateful in itself, whether its consequences be good or evil; few can refuse to admire the courage of those who like More die rather than submit to such an imposition. The ideal of a supranational community to which the individual can appeal from the oppression of local tyranny is one which in both its religious and secular forms has a pressing appeal to the present age.

The English Reformation and Counter-Reformation produced many martyrs both Catholic and Protestant. More remains one of the most attractive of all. Some men, of admirable constancy, almost repel by the way in which they seem to have cultivated martyrdom as a profession; others, however unjust and brutal their sufferings, give the impression that they would have been misfits even in the most humane and tolerant society. More is that rare figure, an Establishment martyr: a man to whom the world and all its promises were open, who had riches and power to hand, which he could have kept if he had been willing to bend to the wind, and who went to his death without bitterness and with a jest. The Utopians would have been proud of him: when a good man dies 'No part of his life is so oft or gladly talked of, as his merry death.'

Suggestions for further reading

(Abbreviations used in references to the works given here are listed at the beginning of the book.)

The standard scholarly edition of More is *The Yale Edition of the Complete Works of St Thomas More* (1963 ff.). Eight volumes of this have appeared, and when it is complete it will include all of More's extant works. Its price puts it beyond the reach of most individual scholars, but fortunately the Yale University Press is also publishing a series of selected works in economic format and modernised spelling. Three of these have been used to provide references in the present work:

St Thomas More: Selected Letters, edited by Elizabeth Frances Rogers (1961)

Utopia, edited by Edward Surtz, SJ (1964)

A Dialogue of Comfort against Tribulation, edited by Frank Manley (1977).

Though I have given page references to Surtz's edition of *Utopia*, I have preferred to quote the earliest translation of Ralph Robinson (1551).

English works of More which have not appeared in these Yale editions are quoted from the unfinished edition of More's works, *The English Works of Sir Thomas More*, of which the first two volumes appeared in 1931 edited by W. E. Campbell and A. W. Reed.

A handy selection of More's writings, including the whole of *Utopia* in translation, is *The Essential Thomas More*, edited by J. J. Greene and John P. Dolan (Mentor-Omega, 1967). I have referred to this from time to time, but have preferred to give my own translations from Latin.

Roper's Life of More is a classic in its own right. It is quoted from the most accessible edition, the Everyman volume edited by E. E.

Reynolds, in which it appears accompanied by Harpsfield's fuller but less vivid Life.

The best modern life of More is still *Thomas More* by R. W. Chambers (Cape, 1935). E. E. Reynolds has written a number of works on More from an explicitly Catholic viewpoint: the fullest is *The Life and Death of St Thomas More* (Burnes and Oates, 1978). Those who find these works excessively hagiographical may discover something more to their taste in the lively but hostile narrative of Jasper Ridley, *The Statesman and the Fanatic* (Constable, 1982).

On *Utopia* there are three books of particular importance: J. H. Hexter, *More's Utopia: The Biography of an Idea* (Princeton, 1952); Edward L. Surtz, *The Praise of Pleasure: Philosophy, Education and Communism in More's Utopia*, and *The Praise of Wisdom: A Commentary on the Religious and Moral Problems and Backgrounds of St Thomas More's Utopia* (both Chicago, 1957).

The most scholarly account of More's judicial and political career is J. A. Guy, *The Public Life of Sir Thomas More* (Harvester, 1980). The best general account of the reign in which his career was set is J. J. Scarisbrick's *Henry VIII* (London, 1968).

An interesting account of More's intellectual career is Alistair Fox's *Thomas More: History and Providence* (Oxford, 1982). This pays particular attention to the controversial writings. A detailed account of both sides of the controversies in which More was engaged is given in R. Pineas, *Thomas More and Tudor Polemics* (Bloomington, Indiana, 1968).

On More's place in the history of English language and literature, see C. S. Lewis, *English Literature in the Sixteenth Century Excluding Drama* (Oxford, 1954). On his place in the humanist movement, see James K. McConica, *English Humanists and Reformation Politics* (Oxford, 1963).

On individual works the valuable introductions to the Yale edition should be consulted; the introductions to *Utopia* by Hexter and Surtz are particularly useful.

A number of the most influential articles of recent years is collected in the anthology edited by R. S. Sylvester and G. Marc'hadour, *Essential Articles for the Study of Thomas More*

(Hamden, Connecticut, 1977). This contains pieces on different aspects of More's life and work by Coulton, Derrett, Elton, McConica and others.

A mine of interesting information about More is to be found in *The King's Good Servant*, by J. B. Trapp and H. S. Herbrüggen, published by the National Portrait Gallery as a catalogue of the exhibition held in 1977 to mark the quincentenary of More's birth.

Index

Index